Helene M. English

HERMAN MELVILLE'S
RELIGIOUS
JOURNEY

HERMAN MELVILLE'S
RELIGIOUS
JOURNEY

Walter Donald Kring

PENTLAND PRESS, INC.
ENGLAND•USA•SCOTLAND

PUBLISHED BY PENTLAND PRESS, INC.
5124 Bur Oak Circle, Raleigh, North Carolina 27612
United States of America
919-782-0281

ISBN 1-57197-053-3
Library of Congress Catalog Card Number 96-71068

Printed in the United States of America

DEDICATION

This work is dedicated to the numberless souls who have questioned their religious background, but who, like Herman Melville, have worked their way through doubt and despair to a reasonable and satisfactory religious belief.

"Let him who seeks continue seeking until he finds. When he finds, he will become troubled. When he becomes troubled, he will be astonished, and he will rule over all."

The Gospel of Thomas (2)

CONTENTS

P R E F A C E

In his introduction to *The Melville Log*, Jay Leyda speaks of "the bog of Melville misinterpretation (with its thick growth of wild guesses.)" Leyda's purpose in compiling *The Melville Log* [1] was to gather together all of the facts that he could find in print as well as unpublished manuscripts in order to counter the misconceptions about Herman Melville. Leyda wrote:

> "Is there anyone in American literature who has attracted such a swarm of myths and apocrypha as has Melville? I mean those statements and whisperings that go beyond 'interpretation'—though this, too, often indulges in such ornamental biography as to verge on fiction. Many of these myths and fancies are the smoke of bonfires in which so many recorded facts of his life have been consumed." [2]

For example, some people who read *Moby-Dick* presume to take Father Mapple's sermon to be Herman Melville's own personal religious thinking, not realizing that Melville may have been putting into his character's mouth a sermon which was merely reminiscent of the sermons which Melville had heard in his boyhood—including one which he may have heard at the Whaler's Chapel in New Bedford.

Further, it is normally assumed that Melville followed the religious tenets of his childhood years, during which he was thoroughly indoctrinated in the neo-Calvinism of the Dutch Reformed Church. Melville's Unitarian-raised father had evidently given up attending a Unitarian church after he married Maria Gansevoort, and, in any case, his children were raised in the Dutch Reformed Church of their mother. Other Melville scholars have sensed very different religious tendencies in Melville's position on Calvinism. Some have called his views humanistic; some have even felt that he had no religious beliefs at all.

Few of the scholars seem to have been impressed with the fact that Herman Melville himself married a Boston *Unitarian*, and that, almost immediately upon their removal to New York City, the couple rented a pew in Dr. Henry Whitney Bellows' All Souls Unitarian Church.

For my part, I have been curious about Herman Melville's religion ever since I discovered in 1975 that he had visited his minister, Bellows' successor, Dr. Theodore Chickering Williams of All Souls Unitarian Church in New York City, around 1884, and had asked that his name be entered as a member of the church, indicating that he had accepted its covenant. Until I found his name in the membership book, I had known little about Herman Melville, and that knowledge was limited to the noted American literary figure. No one had ever suggested to me that Melville might be a Unitarian or a member of All Souls Unitarian Church. As a child, I had read only short portions of *Moby-Dick*. I should add that I am not a bona fide Melville scholar. I hold no professorship in a distinguished English department of any prestigious university. I do not write using the language of the Melville scholars; I know little about Freudian theory which seems to be so rampant in the writings about Melville. I am simply Minister Emeritus of the church that Melville joined during the previous century (having served as the minister from 1955 until 1978).

I happened on Melville's connection with All Souls Unitarian Church in the following manner. I had been doing research at the Massachusetts Historical Society in order to write the first full-length biography of Dr. Henry Bellows, who had served as minister of the church from 1839 until 1882. Bellows was a very significant gentleman of the cloth in his time (1814 - 1882). In addition to preaching forty-three years in a great city pulpit, Bellows also had a great deal of organizing ability. During the Civil War, he was the president of the United States Sanitary Commission, which ministered to the needs of the soldiers and sailors of the Union Army and

Navy and was the forerunner of the American Red Cross. Just before the Civil War ended, Henry Bellows had also lent his organizational skills and prestige to organizing the Unitarian churches of the United States into The National Conference of Unitarian Churches. As it turned out during my research, I discovered that Bellows was also the minister of the Herman Melville family in New York City.

Included in my reading of all of Henry Whitney Bellows' copious correspondence was an exchange of letters between Bellows and his lawyer in Boston, Samuel Shaw, the son of Chief Justice Lemuel Shaw of the Massachusetts Supreme Court, concerning the legal matters of some Bellows' family properties in Boston of which Dr. Bellows was the trustee. Included in the file was a letter dated 6 May 1867, which I simply could not understand. It was from Samuel Shaw to Bellows about his half-sister Elizabeth S. Melville.

Written in response to a letter (now presumably lost) from Bellows in which the minister had informed Shaw that Elizabeth had sought his advice about leaving her husband, the letter indicated that apparently either Bellows or Elizabeth had proposed a staged kidnapping in which Mrs. Melville, seemingly against her will, would be taken from her home and shipped off to live with her half-brother in Boston. The proposal had shocked Samuel Shaw, who stated in his reply to Bellows that, as a lawyer, he did not think that a feigned kidnapping of his sister by some of her friends and her coming to Boston to live with his family was a very good idea.

This letter about kidnapping seemed entirely out of context compared with the other correspondence. I had it copied and put it aside, hoping that some light as to its meaning would be shed at a later date. A week later, I ran across a letter dated 20 May 1867, from an Elizabeth S. Melville to Dr. Bellows thanking him for all of the good advice that he had given her before he had left for a sabbatical in Europe.

Who was this Elizabeth S. Melville? Was there any connection to the American author Herman Melville? Did the two letters have any connection with the H. Melville listed in the All Souls pew rental book?

Further research revealed that Elizabeth S. Melville was Elizabeth Shaw Melville, that she was the daughter of Chief Justice Lemuel Shaw, and half-sister to Samuel Shaw. It also turned out that she was, indeed, the wife of Herman Melville, the famous author of *Moby-Dick*.

I then looked in Dr. Williams' "List of Persons in Congregation of All Souls Church, New York" (which was the list of the actual members of the church as opposed to those who merely rented or owned pews in the church), which is in the possession of All Souls Church. There was the name of Herman Melville, listed as residing at 104 East Twenty-sixth Street in New York City, just six short blocks north of All Souls Church. There could be no doubt that a new fact had been found: Herman Melville, the author, had indeed been a member of a Unitarian church.

The Massachusetts Historical Society published the two letters and a short article about them in *The Massachusetts Historical Society Proceedings*. Somehow, the secretary of the Melville Society, Dr. Donald Yannella, got hold of a reprint of the article, and when the Modern Language Association met in New York City he put a copy in the box of each member of the Melville Society. Dr. Yannella also contacted me, and thus began my acquaintance with many of the country's Melville scholars, and the research into what until then had been to me a rather obscure literary figure.

Eventually in 1981, the Melville Society published *The Endless, Winding Way in Melville: New Charts by Kring and Carey*, edited by two well-known and respected Melville scholars, Donald Yannella and Hershel Parker. This eighty-page booklet reprinted the article from *The Massachusetts Historical Society Proceedings*, and the editors asked a dozen leading Melville scholars to comment on the letters. Their comments on the kidnapping plot make very interesting reading for anyone interested in Melville's life and character; yet in the eleven commentaries that were printed in the booklet, not one of the scholars comments on Melville's *Unitarianism*.

Just how important these two letters have been to those seeking to know more of the personal life of Herman Melville is indicated by the fact that Lynn Horth, the editor of the recently published (1993) Northwestern-Newberry Edition *Correspondence*, includes the two letters, even though they are not by or to Herman Melville himself (page 859). The editor makes the comment that "the two letters are included in this volume because they are more directly and intimately concerned with Melville himself than any other known correspondence within his extended family."

Considering how much has been written on the effects of religion on Melville's life, it was surprising that none of the scholars seemed to be seriously interested in the fact that Melville was a Unitarian. In fact, Melville's connections to Unitarianism had been missed by Unitarians themselves, not a common event in the light of the historically close connection between nineteenth-century American literature and the Unitarian movement. Writing in 1902 about the achievements of nineteenth-century Unitarians, the historian George Willis Cooke, in *Unitarianism in America*, lists the many literary figures whom he considers to be Unitarian.[3] Among the novelists, he lists four Unitarian ministers: Sylvester Judd, William Ware (the first minister at All Souls), Thomas W. Higginson, and Edward Everett Hale, not all well known by modern students of literature. He also lists some who today are giants, and some lesser figures: John T. Trowbridge, Bayard Taylor, Bret Harte, William D. Howells and Nathaniel Hawthorne. Cooke also lists a group of Unitarian women novelists: Catherine Sedgwick (a member of All Souls), Lydia Maria Child, Grace Greenwood, Helen Hunt Jackson, and Harriet Prescott Spofford. Herman Melville's name does not appear in Cooke's list of novelists. Of course, Ralph Waldo Emerson is probably the most famous Unitarian literary figure, although he was not a novelist.

Cooke knows that to name some of these people as Unitarians (many of whom never darkened a church doorway except to attend the funerals of their friends), is a bit risky. But he points out that most of the liberal influences in their lives were brought about by the Unitarian movement which undergirds American religious history from the last part of the eighteenth century right through all of the nineteenth.

It might have been at least *suspected* long ago that Herman Melville became a Unitarian, because Melville's in-laws, the Shaws, as well as his father, were Unitarians. But what about Herman himself? Many scholars have assumed that because what Melville wrote in his books *appeared* to be Calvinistic, Melville was a Calvinist; on the other hand, because Melville indicated no specific religious creed, other scholars have assumed that he professed no formal religion and that he belonged to no specific church. Yet there can be no doubt, as one reads his works, that Melville asked all of the perplexing fundamental questions about life; questions that are traditionally included in the area of religion. Perhaps scholars have missed the point, believing that to be religious one must display an adherence to creeds which recognizably fit into one institutional denomination or another.

When I told the story of this discovery to Dr. James Luther Adams, a prominent Unitarian scholar, he was not surprised. Adams commented that this showed that Unitarianism in the late nineteenth century, as today, was not a monolithic belief, but there was, as today, a great variety of avenues of religious search and opinions among Unitarians.

Some of the Melville scholars still dispute these new findings, disdaining the idea that Melville joined a Unitarian church. They are apt to say that he went to church occasionally with Elizabeth and the children. But these scholars have not studied the by-laws of All Souls Church, which state that to become a member of the church, one must go to the minister and indicate that he wants his name to be entered in the membership book. This act distinguishes a member of the church from a member of the society who merely rents or buys a pew in the church, or otherwise attends services and votes in congregational meetings. It is likely that it was a matter of some conviction on Herman's part to have his name enrolled as a church member.

In the ensuing decade, I became increasingly interested in this stubborn issue of Melville's spiritual life and its development. Since the prevailing scholarly literature was of little help, I began to read Melville's works, including even that gargantuan example of poetry, *Clarel*, the longest poem in the modern English language. In pursuing the events that are known of Melville's life as they juxtapose against the background of the history of religion in America, and relating Melville's writings in these two contexts, I began to see a pattern. It has been a long and arduous search, and this book is the result of that search.

It is not my intention to add to the abundant fictions about Herman Melville, but rather starting from the proven fact of his church membership, to suggest some new possibilities about Melville's personal religious thought and his religious life to the scholarly world, and for the consideration of those who just love Melville for the writer that he was. I suggest that in order to understand both the man and his literary contribution, it is necessary to keep these possibilities in mind. I herewith present some facts which were not known when Jay Leyda published *The Melville Log* in 1969. I will also present some hypotheses which seem reasonable to me, based upon these facts.

I wish to thank the members of the Melville Society who, over the years, have encouraged me to study and to learn more about what church membership meant in Melville's day. To Richard and Rosemary Harris for encouraging me to publish the book. And to my wife, Sage, who suffered through my living so long in the nineteenth century.

Walter Donald Kring
September 1996

CHAPTER ONE

BORN INTO RELIGIOUS CONTROVERSY

Herman Melville was born at a time of great religious fervor and controversy in America. Although scholars of American literature in general, and of the author Herman Melville in particular, have stressed the various concepts that produced the man and his novels, few have taken into account the enormous religious tempest which was raging in the United States at the time of Melville's birth and childhood development.

Herman Melville was born in New York City on 1 August 1819, of good Scottish and Dutch stock. He was delivered by Dr. Wright at Six Pearl Street, the third child and second son of Allan Melvill [1] and Maria Gansevoort Melvill.[2] He was baptized at the home of the Reverend Mr. Matthews of the South Reformed Dutch Church, on 10 August.[3] This was the same clergyman who later baptized Herman's sister, Augusta Melvill, on 24 September 1821, and brother Allan on 16 May 1823. When Catherine arrived in 1825, she was baptized by the Reverend Mr. McLean of the Dutch Reformed Church on Broome Street. From these facts it can be seen that the children of Maria Gansevoort and Allan Melvill were born into the Dutch Reformed Church, the highly Calvinistic denomination of Herman's mother's family.

But Maria Gansevoort and her Dutch Reformed heritage comprise only one half of the religio-cultural influence upon the Melvills' children. Herman's father came from a very different background ethnically, religiously, and culturally, and the contrast and conflict between the two heritages—in many respects, the central conflict in the American nation itself—was to have profound effects on the growing Herman and his writings as an adult. We shall try to explain these two traditions—first that of Herman's mother and then that of his father—to illustrate the strong contrasts with respect to one another, and in respect to the boy who was to become the noted American author.

The New York City into which Herman Melville was born was hardly the present metropolis with all of its skyscrapers and millions of residents, famous Times Square and Central Park. When Melville was born in 1819, the Erie Canal was only in the early stages of building. New York was still a provincial town, along with many other equally important but small cities along the Atlantic Coast. It was the Erie Canal which transformed the superb harbor into an international seaport.

The Dutch had made the first settlement in New York. Manhattan Island was purchased from the Indians in 1626. Two years after the founding of Manhattan, the first minister of the Dutch Reformed Church arrived in 1628. Until the English arrived with their Episcopalian, or Church of England, faith, the Dutch Reformed Church was the predominant denomination on Manhattan Island.

The theological basis of the Dutch Reformed Church, still important at the time that Melville lived, was the theology of John Calvin (1509-1564). Born in France, Calvin was destined for an ecclesiastical career and received the tonsure in 1521. He attended several French universities and studied theology and law. Martin Luther had nailed his thesis on the church door at Wittenberg as an invitation to debate in Germany in 1517, and the Reformation began in earnest.

France, however, was not as quick to revolt against the papacy as the Germans had been. Converted to the new reformers' ideas in 1533, Calvin had a conflict with the French authorities and fled to Basel, Switzerland, then to Geneva. Here he began to study and write about ideas which resulted in the particular theology which came to bear his name. John Calvin became the preeminent theologian of the new Protestant religion.

d. Calvin proposed a stern religious system. His dominant thesis was the infinite and transcendent sovereignty of God. Man's end is to know this God, especially through the Scriptures. But while God is the source of all good, man is corrupt and guilty. Through the fall of Adam, depravity and corruption attach to all men. Thus there resides in every man the curse of the transgression of Adam. This pestilence resides in every generation of mankind; even infants are bound to this corruption by their own fault, and their evil is to be justly punished.

To redeem man from this state of corruption, the Son of God became incarnate. He became prophet, priest, and king, and by his humiliation and suffering ended with his death on the cross, Jesus Christ redeemed mankind from Adam's sin. Christ merited for man the grace of salvation. Yet until man is united to Christ, the benefits of Christ's life and death cannot be attained by him. Joined to Christ, the believer has the life of God in him, and he knows that he is *saved*. Thus he is one of the *elect* of God.

But God has *predestined* human souls for Heaven, or for eternal punishment in Hell. Good works cannot get one who is doomed for Hell into Heaven. Those who are lucky enough to have been pre-chosen for Heaven don't know that they are *chosen* until they have gone through this process. The external means by which God unites men into the fellowship of Christ are the church and its ordinances, especially the Church sacraments of baptism and the Lord's Supper. The ministers of this church are to expound the Scriptures and to reprimand the wayward and the sinners. Everyone is supposed to attend church so that he will discover if he is one of the *elect*.

During Calvin's own lifetime, his doctrines had been attacked. It was especially his doctrine of God and of predestination that was the crux of the criticism. "He held that the world is so governed by God that nothing is done therein but by His *secret counsel and decree*."[4] Many theologians who did not subscribe to the Calvinist doctrines, but who still believed in the sovereignty of God, protested that this idea obliterated the moral freedom that man has to choose good or evil, especially the theory by which some persons were guaranteed salvation while the unfortunate remainder were destined to Hell, and there wasn't much of anything that the damned could do about it.

Apart from the apparent heavenly injustice to this theory, there were rather drastic behavioral implications: anyone could do just as he pleased. If predestined to heaven, no sin could change it, and if predetermined to hell, what was the use to try to do good?

There had been those in the Dutch church who had always been suspicious of this doctrine; chief among these was Jacobus Arminius, a professor at the University of Leyden, who challenged this lack of man's freedom to choose in the system of John Calvin. He claimed that this made God the author of sin, which was unthinkable for a Christian. Arminius gave a series of lectures in 1604 on predestination which challenged Calvin's doctrine. But the Dutch church rejected his challenge and the many later attempts to revive what came to be called Arminianism.

> Arminianism was regarded as nothing less than a blasphemous effort to convict God himself for the common misery in which men have plunged themselves. The liberal effort to soften the doctrines concerning redemption, to qualify God's sovereignty so as to give man some measure of direct control over his eternal fate, was taken as an act of defiance against that sovereignty.[5]

When the British took over Manhattan in 1664, they allowed Calvinism to be practiced openly. The Dutch colony continued to prosper under British rule, and over the next two centuries there remained a proud Dutch aristocracy.

During the eighteenth century, the movement within American religion, later known as the Great Awakening, served to divide the Dutch church into two groups, one—called liberal—favored freedom from the Church of the Netherlands. They supported the revivals of the Great Awakening, hoped to found a college, and wanted the free use of the English language in the churches. The other group

was extremely conservative, wishing to retain as much cohe-
sion with Dutch culture and the original homeland church as
possible. The liberal group grew more rapidly, and founded
Queen's College (later Rutgers University) in 1766.

After the Revolutionary War, the Dutch church became
completely independent. By 1820, the year after Herman
Melville was born, the Dutch language had ceased to be used.
The name Reformed Protestant Dutch Church was changed in
1867 to the Reformed Church in America. The Dutch Church
has continued to thrive over the centuries, and still exists in
Manhattan today in what are called the collegiate churches.
Dr. Norman Vincent Peale was one of the most famous of the
preachers of this denomination. The author's wife's grandfather, Dr. Donald Sage Mackay, was the minister of one of these
churches, St. Nicholas, at the turn of the century: the enormous and impressive building on Fifth Avenue was torn
down in the 1940s to make way for a skyscraper.

Herman Melville's family background was one half—the
Gansevoorts—from this old New York aristocracy. As in most
provincial societies, the family was the most important part of
the New York Dutch social system. There was the legacy of
two hundred years of inherited wealth to bolster up the
importance of these Dutch families.

> They had only to sit tight to be eminent; as the population
> grew, the value of the land doubled and quadrupled, and in spite
> of rent wars and the abolition of feudal privileges, the landed
> families rose to the top like cream.[6]

These Dutch were not especially city dwellers as we conceive them today, but were farmers instead. They farmed from
the environs of New York City up the Hudson by the Tappan
Zee, as far as Saratoga. They lived in commodious stone or
brick houses. So, although Herman Melville was born in New
York City, his familial background on his mother's side of the
family was more rural than urban.

The other half of Herman Melville's family background
came from proud Scottish aristocracy. His grandfather, Major
Thomas Melvill (1751-1832), was of Scottish ancestry and

lived in Boston. His sympathies were typical of Boston liberalism; and he participated in the Boston Tea Party and fought in the Revolutionary War. President George Washington appointed him Collector of the Port of Boston, a political plum.

Thomas Melvill's son, Allan (1782-1832), the father of Herman, grew up in the culturally liberal atmosphere of Boston. As part of this Boston liberalism, there was a strong strain of Arminianism and Unitarianism, which had their influence upon Allan.

New England Unitarianism grew out of Congregationalism largely as Arminianism. The Great Awakening had seen an upsurge of revivalism and emotionalism in religion. This divided the Congregationalists, as the churches near or in Boston tended to reject revivalism; of these churches, those that later became Unitarian tended at this earlier time to be Arminian. On the other hand, many of the churches of western Massachusetts and Connecticut favored emotional conversions; those churches embracing revivalism tended to be anti-Arminian.

The split of the liberals and the conservatives came first over the doctrine of free will; the issue of the unity of God as against the Trinity came later, although, in 1783, the Episcopal King's Chapel revised its Prayer Book to omit all references to the Trinity.

As early as 1785, the First Parish in Worcester, Massachusetts, split over the calling of a successor to Reverend Thaddeus McCarty. A portion of the church members—largely those of the mercantile and professional classes—were liberals, or Arminians. The farmers and others tended to stick to Calvinist orthodoxy. When no agreement could be reached on calling a new minister, the Second Parish split off from the First Parish. The liberal group called Aaron Bancroft (father of the historian George Bancroft) to be their minister. Incidentally, and not coincidentally, Aaron Bancroft was elected to be the first president of the American Unitarian Association which was organized in 1825, after Bancroft had served the Second Parish for forty years.

The Unitarians, whose intellectual fortress was Harvard College, believed the Arminian doctrine that man had some measure of free will; that everything was not predetermined by a fickle God, as in strict Calvinism. These liberals argued that God would not condemn men and women, and especially children, to Hell because they were not of the elect.

Allan Melvill was strongly influenced by the growing foment between Calvinism and Unitarianism. In contrast with the Calvinism of Maria's Dutch Reformed Church, Allan Melvill was "reared with an emphatically positive estimate of human nature and of the promise of life in this world, and he retained these liberal attitudes into maturity."[7] He had a good dose of Unitarian optimism. Allan had originally intended to enter the ministry, and had spent a year in the College of New Jersey, now Princeton University. But he later broke with its Calvinist orthodoxy, and joined the Brattle Square Church in Boston which had called the promising young Reverend Joseph Stevens Buckminster as its minister in 1804 and, after the minister's untimely death, the Reverend Edward Everett, who was later to be president of Harvard College.

Although Buckminster was two years younger than Allan Melvill, he became Allan Melvill's minister. As contemporaries, the two may have had a warm friendship. Certainly Allan respected the Reverend, as he was to turn to his sermons for strength during a grave crisis.

Joseph Stevens Buckminster was born in Portsmouth, New Hampshire in 1784, where his father was the pastor of the North Church. After completing Phillips Exeter Academy in a year, Buckminster entered Harvard College at age twelve where he earned his degree in 1800. He decided on the ministry and was associated with James Freeman at King's Chapel in Boston, which, as previously mentioned, had revised its Church of England Prayer Book to conform to Unitarian beliefs. Then, in 1804, Buckminster was called to the Brattle Street Church in Boston. During a trip to Europe, he gathered a library of three thousand books of British and Continental scholarship, after which he returned to his pastorate to become one of the brilliant liberal voices of Boston

Unitarianism—although it was not called by this name until 1815. Buckminster was a founder of the Boston Athenaeum and was appointed as lecturer on Biblical criticism at Harvard, but he died of an epileptic attack in his twenty-eighth year.

Meanwhile, Allan Melvill had joined the ranks of the merchants as an importer of French goods. He was overpowered in his thinking about the importance of the material amenities of life. At age thirty-two, he married Maria, a daughter of the wealthy Gansevoorts of Albany. Had he not married into this family, the father of the future novelist might not otherwise have been associated with the Dutch Reformed Church. Interestingly, "neither Allan Melvill nor his wife Maria formally belonged to the Dutch Reformed Church, but Maria had been reared in the church as a member of the mighty Gansevoort clan of Albany."[8]

For this reason—and for the fact that it was the more conservative religious view which prevailed as socially correct—it was decided between Allan and Maria that the children should be raised in the orthodox Dutch Church rather than in the more liberal and rapidly changing Congregational (Unitarian) faith.

As fate would have it, only four months before Maria gave birth to her third child, Herman, the now famous—or infamous, at the time—William Ellery Channing had spoken informally to a small group that had gathered in his sister's New York City residence only a few short city blocks from where Herman Melville was born. Channing had attained fame virtually overnight in 1815, when he had distinguished himself as the first Congregational minister to come out openly to use the word Unitarian concerning his own theological views. While the Protestant orthodoxy was shocked and most displeased, Channing had ever since gained an increased following. Now Channing was on his way to fulfill an invitation from the Baltimore church to speak at the service of the ordination of Jared Sparks, where he would deliver his famous Baltimore sermon. In this sermon, Channing implied that the orthodox faith was a faith for "cripples."

On his return trip to Boston, Channing again stopped over at his sister's, and preached to throngs of New York City's interested. It was out of these two New York stopovers that a group of New York laymen (mostly those who had originated in New England) organized the First Congregational Church of New York City, an openly Unitarian society, on 24 May 1819. The church was incorporated under New York state law on 15 November 1819, and later became known as the Unitarian Church of All Souls. This would later turn out to be Herman Melville's own church.

Channing believed that most of the Calvinistic doctrines were offensive to human dignity. He actually believed in the literal inspiration of the Scriptures, but he read the Scriptures with a very different eye than that of his Calvinist brethren. He believed that the doctrine of the Trinity was simply un-Biblical. Channing refused to abdicate his rational dignity before the inscrutable glory of a Calvinist God.

It is perhaps portentous to the fate of American literature that Unitarianism gained its roots in New York City the very year that Herman Melville was born.

In contrast to the long standing inherited wealth of the Gansevoorts, Allan Melvill was a struggling merchant, but Herman's birthplace, Number Six Pearl Street, was then a fashionable New York City neighborhood. The house soon became too small for a family of five children, however, especially with more on the way, so when Herman was five (1824), the family moved further uptown to a rented home on Bleeker Street.

Herman's mother, apparently, was vain and narcissistic, emphasizing the material aspects of life.

> She was correct, formal, proud; she valued a high station in life, to which her maiden name, at least, entitled her; she valued good food, low voices, courteous servants, correct manners . . . and to the last she wore her pride in station like a crest.[9]

In an early biography of Melville (1929), Lewis Mumford, describes the family as stilted and artificial.

Both Melville's father and his mother were monsters; but it took him a long time to discover this, because they were correct and meritorious members of society. . . . In New York of the early nineteenth century, Mr. and Mrs. Allan Melvill can be duplicated many times over. Their correctness, their pettiness, their shallowness, were the correctness and shallowness of a venial society whose pretensions to culture and civilization were, on the whole, pretty thin.[10]

In such a family, there may not have been enough parental attention to meet the needs of all of Allan and Maria's children. In any case, Herman was an introverted child who enjoyed reading more than playing outdoors.

Herman and his elder brother Gansevoort were sent to a private school, the New York Male High School.[11] It was run on an English method of education in which the master instructed a small group of the brightest students, and then in turn, each of these monitors instructed a group of eight in the lesson that they had just completed. Although Allan thought that Gansevoort was the brightest of his boys, he was surprised when Herman was chosen to be a monitor.

During his childhood, Herman loved to visit his uncle, Thomas Melvill, Jr., his father's older brother, at a farm named "Broadhall" near Pittsfield, Massachusetts. Uncle Thomas had made a fortune in Paris and on one of his trips (1802) had married a French wife, Francoise Raymonde Eulogie Marie des Douleurs Lame Fleury, the adopted daughter of a French banker. One daughter had issued from this union. But the marriage soon ended in Francoise's death in 1814, and Uncle Thomas lost his fortune. He married again, and it was this second wife that young Herman knew at "Broadhall." Uncle Thomas dodged debtors for the rest of his life. He was imprisoned several times for his debts, much to the chagrin of his father and brothers. He was totally unsuited to run the farm in Pittsfield.

By 1828, Allan had moved up a bit in the mercantile world, and the family moved to a house on Broadway, more commodious than the Bleeker Street home. In spite of the move, the Melvills continued to attend divine service on Broome

Street. Herman was now nine. The Reverend Jacob Brodhead, who was called to the Broome Street Church in 1826, became intimately acquainted with the Melvill family. His children played with the Melvill children.

Herman's earliest religious ideas would have been shaped by this minister. Jacob Brodhead was well known for his style of preaching which attempted to regenerate the souls of his listeners. He was not known for the cold severity commonly associated with Calvinistic ministers, but was "affectionately considerate of the young, and delighting to take little children up in his arms."[12] Instead of emphasizing many of the more barren Calvinistic doctrines, Brodhead emphasized the struggle of every human being to save his own soul. He was also in sympathy with the early message of the Great Awakening; by this time, the Dutch church had a tradition of evangelical pietism. The Dutch church was a strong mover in the search for this new pietism. But the church maintained a strong and unyielding orthodoxy in the midst of this movement.

> In true Calvinistic fashion, Brodhead talked about the domination of sin over human beings, and the power of the Gospel to bring one up from this sin. "Having that almost instinctive skill to reach the more sensitive chords of the human heart, he could not restrain his emotion while he probed the torpid conscience or applied the balm of Gilead to the bleeding spirit."[13]

It was on Calvinistic doctrines such as this that Herman Melville was raised. Like most good young boys of the Dutch Reformed faith, Herman must have accompanied his parents to church often, and must have heard these teachings of Calvinism and of the sinfulness of mankind preached excessively. Thus, Herman was brought up under a modified Calvinism which was drummed into him Sunday after Sunday. It took him years to get over the sense of guilt that had been instilled into him as a young boy.

Some have suggested that Reverend Brodhead might have been the inspiration for Father Mapple, whose sermon in *Moby-Dick* Herman Melville may have dredged up from his boyhood memories. Brodhead preached often on Scriptural narratives and, of course, the sermon in *Moby-Dick* is based upon one of the best yarns in the Bible, the story of Jonah in the belly of the great fish. T. Walter Herbert Jr., writes that:

In *Moby-Dick* he shapes Father Mapple's character and his sermon in accordance with the style of orthodox spirituality Brodhead displayed. As he came to repudiate the religious concepts upon which it was founded, Melville continued to be impressed by the personal force that such an integrity can project, dramatizing it at length in Captain Ahab's monomania. Indeed, Melville's quest portrays the heroism of a man without a standard of final belief, who casts himself unreservedly into the search for it. He seeks a unified vision of ultimate reality that can gather all experience into an intelligible and coherent totality.[14]

As indicated earlier, by the time that Herman Melville was old enough to understand Jacob Broadhead's sermons, the tenets of Calvinism had been somewhat moderated from the beliefs of their founder. Calvinism was still rigorously intellectual, but certain of the doctrines had fallen into obscurity, while others were particularly emphasized:

Just as a mathematician, or indeed any attentive reader of philosophy, may be entranced by the felicity with which stage follows stage in the unfolding symmetry of proof, so the Protestant rationalists of the Calvinist tradition responded to an absorbing intellectual charm and took it as a signal that the divine presence was revealing itself . . . [Melville] exploits traditional religious concepts for the sake of conveying his own untraditional apprehension of the real. His early introduction to the major issues of Calvinistic controversy has an enlarged significance because he was exposed not merely to their substance but to the reverence with which they were handled.[15]

But the innocence of the child who was absorbing these doctrines was to be abruptly broken. Just two years after the family had moved to Broadway, an economic depression hit Allan Melvill's import business hard. Unable to keep up appearances, the Melvill family was forced to abandon New York City.

The family moved to Albany in the fall of 1830 where Allan made a pittance working as a clerk in a fur store. Uncle Peter

Gansevoort was a trustee of the Albany Academy, and so young Herman attended this school, showing promise, not in the classics, which was the backbone of the curriculum, but in mathematics; he carried off the prize. What this schooling also revealed was that Herman was fond of books, and reading became his second nature. Unlike many of the American authors who succeeded in this creative period of American literature, Melville did not go to college. After the move from New York City, Herman's education was sporadic, at best. He never finished high school. But his love of books made him one of the best self-educated men of his day. And even today, as one reads his works, one is amazed at the breadth and depth of his reading as displayed in his writings.

The misfortune of Allan Melvill's bankruptcy had severe effects on each member of the family. Allan continually borrowed money from his father, and when Major Melville died, Allan received nothing. Although Maria inherited some money from the widow of Peter Gansevoort, which helped matters a little, the family was in terrible financial straits. In his misery, Allan evidently turned to a volume of sermons written by his old friend and minister, Joseph Buckminster. After Buckminster's death in 1828, some three years earlier, some of his parishioners had published these sermons. In them, Buckminster expounded the idea that "calamities, though they may wear the guise of punishments, are never administered solely for the sake of punishment, but of correction."[16] In other words, they are part of God's plan for the improvement of the human state of being.

During this period, Allan also read his Bible. He marked two verses of Psalm 55: "My heart is sore pained within me, and the terrors of death are fallen upon me. Fearfulness and trembling are come upon me and horror hath overwhelmed me."[17]

To add to the family's woes, Herman's father's health failed. He caught pneumonia shortly after Christmas the following year. Allan went into a delirium and died two weeks later, on 31 January 1832. Maria had him laid to rest in the

Dutch Church section of the common burying ground. Herman was only twelve years old.

In *Moby-Dick and Calvinism*, T. Walter Herbert, Jr., develops in a chapter titled "A Unitarian Tragedy" the interesting theory that Allan Melvill's Unitarian beliefs had something to do with his misfortune and death from a fever. Herbert believes that "Allan Melvill's faith assisted him in preserving fatal delusions about himself and his world."[18]

The author then goes on to develop the thesis that

> Allan's downfall was played out in terms provided by specific religious traditions; it was a tragedy in which liberal belief conspired with moral failure to bring on bankruptcy, madness, and death.[19]

Herbert concludes that Allan "erected a house of cards, thanking God incessantly for its preservation."[20]

Whether Allan's death was due to the failure of his theological system or not is a moot point. A theological system is seldom developed by individuals, even by those who enter the religious professions. Individuals tend to develop ways of looking at life, including different ways to confront tragedy and loss. Conventional theologies can color each world view, even alter it under certain conditions. But it is unlikely that a conventional religion can *cause* one's state such as Allan's failure and the family's tragedies. What happened to Allan Melvill was due more to his personal way of looking at and dealing with life than to an intellectual theological system; it may even be doubted that he had one. Unitarianism did not teach lethargy or materialism; Boston and New York social life did. These became parts of Allan's character, and they can scarcely be blamed on any conventional theological system as they were by Herbert in calling Allan's death "a Unitarian tragedy." Allan's failure was probably a personal failure; not a theological one.

Allan's death now left the large family in abject poverty, and they were literally thrown upon the welfare of the Gansevoort family. Herman's older brother, Gansevoort, tried to support the family by opening a hat store in Albany.

Herman left school to work as a clerk in the New York State Bank. After working in the bank for just two years, Herman gave up his position and went to live with his Uncle Thomas in Pittsfield. Here he worked as a farm hand for nearly a year. In 1835, he returned home and enrolled in Albany Classical School. One of his teachers remembered Herman as an ardent writer of themes. He also joined the debating society.

His older brother started a fur business, and at this time added the final "e" on *Melville*. The entire family adopted the new spelling, and Herman has been Herman Melville ever since. But the beleaguered family was to suffer more shock. The great depression of 1837 drove Gansevoòrt into bankruptcy. Gansevoort also had a nervous collapse at this time which sidelined him for nearly a year. Unable to afford to live even in Albany, the family moved to Lansingburgh, a town on the Hudson River ten miles north of Albany. Herman again dropped school to help the family finances by teaching in a country school near Pittsfield. But he gave this up at the end of the school year, when he returned home to take a course in surveying, hoping to get work on the Erie Canal. This dream did not materialize either, but Herman did have his first writing published at this time, a small sketch in a Lansingburgh newspaper called "Fragments from a Writing Desk."

Herman did not early get over his grief concerning his father's death. As a young boy, he had idolized his father as a complete man, perhaps a model on which he could form his own life and personality. It was difficult for the adolescent to make sense of Allan's tragic fate. Did the youth now begin to blame his father for abandoning him? Did he resent his father's failure in business and leaving the family in poverty? Did he blame his mother to any degree? Young Herman must have raised many questions regarding what had led to these disasters which had made his young life so miserable.

These years from twelve to twenty are impressionable ones in a man's life; further, it is during the late teens that one normally questions what he has absorbed as a child. For Herman, the dramatic contrast between the seemingly smooth and happy days of his childhood and what came about to bring them to such an abrupt halt caused profound questions about his parents' life and life style in New York City.

Later, Herman was to resolve these conflicts in *Pierre*, which is, in a sense, a novel about his own family. The story ends up as a repudiation of human relationships generally. Melville makes Pierre's father guilty of a secret sin: He has had a child by a young woman before his marriage. By this means, Melville provides a tangible, concrete reason for repudiating his father, rather than an abstract theological, philosophical, or psychological one. In this way, Melville also provides a rational explanation for his father's sudden and seemingly meaningless death. This literary expression is something like the secret sin of Hester Prynne in Nathaniel Hawthorne's *The Scarlet Letter*, which uses the vehicle of adultery to probe the meaning of the Puritan society.

But this resolution actually ends up to be no solution at all, for Pierre eventually out of pity marries the offspring of his father's folly. No individual comes out well in *Pierre*. In this work, Melville spews out the venom of his teens and perhaps retrospectively of his childhood. All of the Glendinnings (read Melvills) turn out to be beasts; the novel manifests Melville's near total disillusionment with family matters and his lack of belief in the veracity of human character. But in another sense, *Pierre* implies that Herman was, at the same time, trying to validate the Calvinistic concept that all people are sinners and cannot escape the results of their sins.

In his tormented teen years, Herman must have been forced to wonder what role his parents' religious views had played in bringing on their hardship. Herbert wrote:

As the paradoxical elements in Herman's religious education ceased to make sense in a coherent totality, he found himself incapable of seeing moral experience intelligibly in theocentric terms. The disaster provided the impetus and the themes for an endless round of agonized meditations in Melville's adult life.[21]

For her part, Herman's prideful mother reacted to her husband's death and the worsening financial problems by joining the First Reformed Dutch Church of Albany only a few months after burying him. According to Calvinism, if one could recognize the sovereignty of God, one was offered a profound solace. Maria declared that she had received God's saving grace; she acknowledged her own helplessness and unworthiness (a tenet of the faith of Calvinism). Then being admitted "on examination and confession of . . . faith,"[22] she was accepted into the church on 6 April 1832. She had not belonged to the church earlier, but now after Allan's death she sought comfort in doctrinal study. Later in 1837 and 1838, two of her daughters, Melville's sisters, Helen and Augusta, also joined the Dutch Reformed Church; Helen on 13 July 1837, and Augusta on 11 October 1838, when they were twenty and seventeen, respectively.

Herbert suggests that this open and complete embracing of Calvinism by his mother and sisters had an influence on the boys' own religious thinking: "Herman was now under pressure to accept the orthodox faith, but as he explored its application to his own experience, he would soon have encountered a painful difficulty."[23]

In any case, it appears that Herman did not follow the example of his mother and sisters. Why we do not know, except that perhaps his doubts—which were later to become so strong—were beginning to surface, and the battle that was going on within his mind about freedom, sin, and predestination were forming the opinions that he was later so strongly to express. But we can only guess about the answers as to his thinking during these critical years.

Channing had predicted that the Calvinistic orthodoxy would collapse within itself. He believed that it was not a doctrine that the new democratic American would be expected to believe. The conflict was between the Calvinistic vision of a humanity doomed to sin except by blind acceptance of Christ by the pre-chosen; and the Unitarian vision of an inherently good humanity which, enacting in *deed* the *teachings* of Jesus earned its rightful place with God. In changes of opinion, this conflict would work its way out in human consciousness.

This conflict certainly has had no easy solution. It began in the American culture at just about the same time Herman

Melville was born; Melville's own family was a microcosm of this conflict, and Herman's entire adult life and his literature are as if a millemicrocosm on the same theme. Melville struggled as a youth, and struggled through the remainder of his adult life until, as we shall see, he made personal and literary peace with the Unitarian Church and with God, through his own personal discoveries.

In the meantime, in 1838, when his prospect of working on the Erie Canal failed, Herman was faced with a more practical problem, one more immediately imperative of solution than all of the large questions that his mind was asking about existence. What was he to do with himself to apply his energies to earning a living and becoming independent of his family?

In the first half of the nineteenth century, before the advent of the railroad, it was accepted practice by the socially elite and poor families alike that their youth would seek their fortunes at sea, and thereby apprentice—not necessarily for seafaring, but for the mercantile and import trades. Many wealthy and socially prominent citizens of the nation had gotten their start in this way. Signing on as a ship hand was an excellent way to see the world and to get experience in the art and science of living. Several of Herman's own cousins had gone to sea. Herman, avid reader that he was, had read Richard Henry Dana's *Two Years Before the Mast*. Herman's fate was sealed when his brother Gansevoort got him a job on a ship that was sailing to Liverpool. On 3 June 1839, Herman signed on as a *boy* on the *St. Lawrence*, a packet ship which plied the route between New York City and Liverpool, England.

C H A P T E R   T W O

DISILLUSIONMENT

What sort of religious thoughts was Herman Melville pondering when he shipped to Liverpool at the age of twenty? In the light of his later disillusionment and cynicism about religious matters, it would seem probable that his questioning mind was already asking for more answers than his young adult mind could find. As an avid reader, Melville seems to have been in pursuit of the ultimate theological questions—questions which he later posed in *Clarel*—to which he found so few satisfactory answers. But the process through which his thinking went must have been typical of the young person who rebels against creedal dogma and becomes an atheist, until he discovers that atheism, too, is a dogmatic stand in religion.

Herman Melville tells the story of his first voyage and the return voyage to New York City in his novel *Redburn* which, although not autobiographical, is certainly quasi-autobiographical. It must be remembered that *Redburn* was not written until after Melville had had his tour of duty on board several whalers in the South Seas, and a tour of duty in the United States Navy, as well. But the impressions that he had on this voyage were lasting, and he easily wrote about them ten years later, in 1849.

The *St. Lawrence* sailed on 5 June 1839. She was a small three-masted, square-rigged ship of some 356 tons, just six years old and in good condition, but a slow ship. Most packet ships made the run to Liverpool in two weeks, but it took the *St. Lawrence* four long weeks to make the trip. Melville found the names of the different parts of the ship strange, and his fellow sailors must have laughed at his ignorance. But he soon learned the sailor's vocabulary which he easily used all of the rest of his life.

It didn't take long after his ship docked in Liverpool for Melville to realize that the docks were in what had become the poorest, worst crime-infested, and most run-down part of the city. Liverpool exemplified the blight of the Industrial Revolution. In the "vicinity of the docks there are many painful sights."[1] Melville was given shore leave, and in order to get to his boarding house, it was necessary for him to make his way through a narrow street called Launcelott's Hey. He described this street as "lined with dingy, prison-like cotton warehouses."[2] Once, in passing through this place he "heard a feeble wail which seemed to come out of the earth."[3] He wrote that he could almost have run when he heard that sound. "It seemed the low, hopeless, endless wail of someone forever lost."[4] He advanced towards the opening from whence came the sound, and there

> some fifteen feet below the walk, crouching in nameless squalor, with her head bowed over, was the figure of what had been a woman. Her blue arms folded to her livid bosom two shrunken things like children, that leaned toward her, one on each side. At first I knew not whether they were alive or dead. They made no sign; they did not move or stir, but from the vault came that soul-sickening wail.[5]

Finally, one of the children lifted its head, and the woman also gazed up at Melville's face peering down at her.

> They were dumb and next to dead with want. How they had crawled into that den, I could not tell, but there they had crawled to die. At that moment I never thought of relieving them; for death was so stamped in their glazed and unimploring eyes, that I almost regarded them as already no more.[6]

Then Melville stopped two "ragged old women" who were groping amid the filthy rubbish, finding little particles of dirty cotton which they washed and sold for a trifle. Melville asked these women if they knew who the three in the pit might be. He asked one of the women if there was not a place "to which the woman might be taken."[7]

"Yes," she replied, "to the church-yard," thinking that the woman was already dead. She had been down there with nothing to eat for three days. One of the old hags said that she deserved her fate, for she had never married. Stopping a policeman, Melville asked if there was not something that could be done, to which the officer replied that this was not his street. Finally the policeman said to Melville, "There, now Jack, go on board your ship and stick to it, and leave these matters to the town."

Melville asked a lot of other people if something couldn't be done. They all gave him the same kind of evasive answer. It was none of their business, people said. The next day, Melville dropped down some bread to the three sufferers. But the next day when he went past he saw that the bread had not been touched. They were dead.

Herman Melville found the same excuses and indifference when he inquired of the policeman and of town officials about the hapless family's burial. It was none of his or their business. Melville was appalled.

He was also appalled at the number of beggars in the streets. Near the ships on the docks where the sailors were discharged for their shore leave, a long line of beggars and professional thieves would congregate. Melville commented, "The first time I passed through this long lane of pauperism, it seemed hard to believe that such an array of misery could be furnished by any town in the world."[8] He discovered, too, that many made a racket out of the bad situation. The ship's cooks, for example, saved all of the old scraps from the kitchen and then sold them on the docks, Melville says, for as much as thirty or forty dollars. Some of the scraps had been saved from a six-month sail.

Melville further described this paupers' line:

Old women, rather mummies, drying up with slow starving and age; young girls, incurably sick, who ought to have been in the hospital; sturdy men, with the gallows in their eyes . . . and a whining lie in their mouths; young boys, hollow-eyed and decrepit; and puny mothers, holding up puny babes in the glare of the sun, formed the main features of the scene.[9]

In the beggars' desperate appeals for charity,

> They beset you on every hand; catching you by the coat; hanging
> on, and following you along; and, *for Heaven's sake* and *for God's*
> *sake*, and *for Christ's sake*, beseeching of you but one ha'penny. If
> you so much as glanced your eye on one of them, even for an
> instant, it was perceived like lightning, and the person never left
> your side until you turned into another street, or satisfied his
> demands. Thus, at least, it was with the sailors; though I
> observed that the beggars treated the town's people differently.[10]

His heart went out to those who suffered such poverty, but he found that most people accepted the suffering as the lot or fate of the poor. The conditions were so much worse than the worst he had known in his own family, which at the time, contrasted with the affluent days of his childhood, had seemed terrible enough. This contrast must have been something of a lesson in humility for young Melville, although the experience was to embark him on a journey of disillusionment with Western Civilization. We shall return to some of Melville's deep feelings of horror at the conditions of the poor in the slums in Liverpool when we discuss the thread of humanism that runs through several of his novels.

Melville did not return to New York City until 1 October 1839. Back in Lansingburgh, Herman was discouraged to discover that the family's economic plight was even worse than when he had gone to sea. Although eager to see his family again, he discovered that mortgages which his mother had signed were being foreclosed; even her furniture was listed for sale by her creditors. Some of this furniture was saved from sale by her brother Peter. Seeking to help with a job of his own, Herman found that the best available position was teaching in a school with sixty pupils in one room in Greenbush, New York. But the school closed before the end of the term and Herman was paid only enough to cover his expenses. He then substituted in another school near Lansingburgh, but by now he was convinced that school teaching was not for him.

An alternative was suggested by his Uncle Thomas (Melvill). One of Uncle Thomas's sons had gone to Galena, Illinois, a frontier community where lead had been discovered in abundance. Uncle Thomas encouraged Herman to try his luck in Galena, perhaps starting out by teaching school there until something more to his liking turned up in the prospering town. Reluctantly, Herman traveled to the west, but after spending several weeks searching in vain for work in Galena, he returned home in what was by now becoming an ingrained discouraged frame of mind.

In November 1840, Herman headed back to New York City hoping to find another job aboard ship. While waiting for a ship, he worked temporarily as a copyist in a lawyer's office. This experience provided the background to write one of his best short stories, "Bartleby, the Scrivener," about a copyist in a lawyer's office who turns inward, and eventually shuts off completely from the outside world—another sign of Melville's growing disillusionment with society and his own insecurity within it.

Of course, Herman felt confined by this office work. Unable to find work aboard a ship similar to the *St. Lawrence*, he decided to seek a whaling ship. The center of the whaling industry was in Massachusetts, notably at New Bedford and Nantucket, so Herman Melville headed for Massachusetts. On the day after Christmas of 1840, he signed papers to be an able-bodied seaman aboard the *Acushnet*. He had spent the previous weekend in New Bedford; on Sunday, he had struggled through the high winds of a sleet storm to hear Reverend Enoch Mudge preach at the Seaman's Bethel Chapel. Reverend Mudge was a seaman's preacher who used all kinds of references to the sea in his sermons. Melville would recount this experience in *Moby-Dick*. Ishmael, too, spent the weekend before signing on to a whaling ship (the *Pequod*) in New Bedford; Ishmael, too, had struggled through a sleet storm to the Whaler's Chapel to hear Father Mapple's well known sermon on Jonah and the whale.[11]

The *Acushnet* was a new ship of 358 tons displacement. It had two decks, three masts, and a square stern. The crew list contained this information: Herman Melville; birthplace New York; age twenty-one; height five feet nine and a half inches; complexion dark; hair brown.[12] He was given advance pay of eighty-four dollars so that he might buy necessities for the trip which might extend for as long as three years.

Although Captain Pease was not as extreme as the one-legged Captain Ahab of the fictitious *Pequod* in *Moby-Dick*, he was tyrannical, autocratic, and arbitrary. Melville also found the conditions on board the ship to be squalid. Whaling could be a nasty, dirty, and dangerous business. The crew were a rough lot, in many cases castaways from prisons and those escaping from something unpleasant back home. With this lot aboard, the *Acushnet* cruised leisurely looking for whales in the South Atlantic, sailed around Cape Horn to look for whales for several months near the Galapagos Islands (with very poor results), and then sailed across the Pacific Ocean to the Marquesas Islands.

The Marquesas, an archipelago consisting of eleven islands, were first discovered in 1595, the first islands of what later came to be called French Oceania to be made known to the outside world. They are the archipelago of French Oceania nearest to the equator. Of volcanic origin, they consist of many valleys surrounded by high mountains running from the interior to the sea. The nature of the terrain dictated that there be separated communities in these valleys.

It was a momentous time in history when the *Acushnet* dropped anchor in the Marquesas, for in the spring of 1842, France was busy annexing islands in the South Pacific. Melville was not aware of this fact until he saw French battleships anchored in the harbor in the bay of Nuku Hiva. The tricolor of France trailed over the sterns of six black-hulled vessels. The whole group of islands had been taken possession of by Rear Admiral Du Petit-Thouars in the name of France. Subsequent events that summer would focus Melville's mind against the whole idea of colonialism waged by military power, which provided one of the strong anti-Western themes in his novels.

But what interested the sailors of the *Acushnet* more than the French battleships was the greeting which the ship received from the natives from the shore. A flotilla of brown men arrived in outrigger canoes, and some men swam out to the ship. Then came a sight of which the sailors had long dreamed, the sight of the whinhenies, or more properly, the *wahines*, or Polynesian women, who reached the deck by climbing up the anchor ropes and the ladders. They all reached the deck in one way or another, "dripping with the brine and glowing from the bath, their jet-black tresses streaming over their shoulders, and half enveloping their otherwise naked forms."[13] They dried each other off with white tapa cloth and anointed their bodies with oil.

That evening these mermaids showed off their natives dances, and Melville wrote that they danced with "an abandoned voluptuousness" which he did not dare to describe further. "Although in *Typee* he would moralize on the corruption of these unsophisticated 'savages' by 'civilized' white men, he left no doubt how he and his fellow whalers responded to these winsome tempters."[14]

The Marquesans are a handsome and charming people, and are among the taller and the lighter-skinned Polynesians. They grew taro, coconuts, breadfruit, and other tropical fruits and vegetables in their isolated little communities. At the time of their discovery, the population was estimated at a hundred thousand persons, but the numbers declined precipitously to several thousands after contact with the white man's diseases and his culture.

There were rumors adrift on the *Acushnet* that some of the natives of the Marquesas were cannibals. These supposedly lived up in the Typee Valley. Several of the men talked about visiting the Typee Valley to see the cannibals. The fact that they were reputed to eat human flesh did not seem to deter Melville, who saw in this an opportunity to desert ship. He had been on board the *Acushnet* for eighteen long months, and had had enough of whaling to suit his fancy. He resented the captain's tyranny, the neglect of the welfare of the crew, and the near starvation fare of poor-quality food that was fed to the sailors. Even peril at the hands of cannibals seemed mild compared to life on the whaling ship. Herman found a companion in a small shipmate his own age named Richard Tobias Greene, called Toby by his shipmates. Together they plotted an escape from the ship and a visit to the Typee Valley.

The sailors were to have shore leave on 9 July 1842, and the night before, the two would-be deserters accumulated some sea biscuits and gathered a few things to barter with the natives. Shortly after they stepped ashore, a torrential tropical rain gave the two deserters a chance to slip away while their companions dozed in the shelter of a boathouse. As the story is told in *Typee*—*written* in 1846, some four years later— Melville was traveling with a swollen leg. After six days[15] of climbing over treacherous terrain, he and Toby arrived at the Typee Valley. Here they were met by natives who did not appear to be cannibalistic at all. In the novel, *Tomo*, the lead character who represents Melville, lived here for four months. Herman and Toby even learned to converse in the native language.[16]

Melville compares life in the Typee valley to life as he knew it in America and Europe. "In this secluded abode of happiness there were no cross old women, no cruel stepdames, no withered spinsters, no love-sick maidens, no sour old bachelors, no inattentive husbands, no melancholy young men, no blubbering youngsters, and no squalling brats. All was mirth, fun, and good high humor. Blue devils, hypochondria, and doleful dumps, went out and hid themselves among the nooks and crannies of the rocks."

For Melville, this experience among the non-civilized was an eye opener on how life *could* be, and probably even *should* be, as it is a natural life rather than one filled with artifice, as European culture was. As summarized by Gay Wilson Allen,

the world of the Typees was an almost unconscious world in which the fruit of the tree of knowledge had not yet been eaten. The Typees were not acquisitive, either for knowledge or things, beyond their easily satisfied needs. Food grew on trees, or in the ocean not too far away, and they needed little clothing or shelter. They had time to enjoy eating, singing, being sociable, and making love. It was as near paradise as Herman Melville ever came, and he would never be the same again.[17]

Of course, Melville did not plan to remain among the Typees forever. Yet the natives made it apparent that they did not want their visitors to leave! Toby Greene managed to slip away from the Typees to try to get help escaping, and located an Australian whaler, the *Lucy Ann*. Reporting on his friend's stranding among the Typees, Toby persuaded the sailors from this ship to row a longboat to the Typee Valley. Thus, Herman Melville was rescued from the reluctant natives. He joined the sailors as an able seaman on the *Lucy Ann*. Here the story as related in *Typee* ends.

The perennial question among scholars has always been whether *Typee* is fiction or fact. When it was published, much criticism ensued about the contents of the book (especially the passages about the Christian missionaries). There was an attempt to prove that the events had actually not occurred. Fortunately, Tobias Greene read a review of the book and came forward to substantiate the fact that he had accompanied Herman Melville on such a trip. Perhaps Harrison Hayford sums the matter up best:

Although we have misgivings about the veracity of many parts of the story, we do know that [Melville] visited the Marquesas Islands for one month, though we do not know exactly how he spent that time, and the general outlines of the Melville story may still be credited. After deserting the ship he did cross the mountains with Toby, did descend into the Typee valley and live there for a while. Perhaps the more romantic aspects of his story are exaggerations of his actual experiences. Such instances are the length and difficulties of crossing the mountain and descending the cliffs, a trip later visitors say need have taken only three or four hours, was only four or five miles long, and could have been made on a well-worn native path; another exaggeration is the intensity of his fear of being eaten or tattooed.[18]

Most scholars seem to agree that Tomo's relationship with the beautiful Polynesian damsel Fayaway is probably fiction. But the kindness of the savages impressed Melville.

Later, Herman Melville would write his second book about his South Seas adventures, *Omoo*. The word *omoo* in Polynesian means wanderer or rover, or person wandering from one island to another, which is what Melville himself was doing during this period of his life. The book is an auto-biographical narrative which begins when Melville escaped from the Typee Valley and boarded the *Lucy Ann*.

Melville contracted for one cruise on the *Lucy Ann* which, under a Captain Venton, headed for the whaling grounds in the seas around Japan. But Captain Venton, although a young man, became so ill that he ordered his ship to sail to the nearest island group of Tahiti. The Captain was taken ashore, leaving his first mate James German in charge of the ship. The crew hated this man and resisted his authority. Fifteen of the sailors—including Herman Melville—signed a letter directed to the British consul which stated that they would not serve under German. As a consequence, they were all arrested and put aboard the French warship *La Rein Blanche* in chains.

But luck was to be with them; in a few days the sailors were turned over to a good-natured Tahitian marshal called Captain Bob. The orders were for the men to be placed in jail, but the only furniture of the jail were stocks which secured the men's legs so that they could not escape. Captain Bob put the men in the stocks at night, but let them run free about the prison grounds most of the daytime. Thus, except for having to report daily to Captain Bob, Melville had an opportunity to do what he wanted and to observe the native customs. One Sunday morning, Captain Bob reported that the *Lucy Ann* had left the harbor. Now the prisoners were allowed to roam the entire island as they wished. Melville had made friends with the ship's doctor, who also had refused to serve under German. In *Omoo*, Melville called the doctor Long Ghost. With the doctor as a companion, Melville became a beach boy, first at Papeete, and then on other Tahitian islands.

The island paradise of Tahiti is where the story of *Omoo* takes place. One of the places the two men liked to visit was the Royal Mission Chapel, which is described in *Omoo*.

[The Royal Mission Chapel at Papoar] was over seven hundred feet in length, and of a proportionate width; the vast ridge-pole was, at intervals, supported by a row of thirty-six cylindrical trunks of the bread-fruit tree; and, all around, the wall-plates rested on shafts of the palm. The roof—steeply inclining to within a man's height of the ground—was thatched with leaves, and the sides of the edifice were open . . . a considerable brook, after descending from the hills and watering the valley, was bridged over in three places, and swept clean through the chapel.[19]

Melville listened to a sermon which had very little substance, and he remarked,

Such was the substance of a great part of this discourse; and, whatever may be thought of it, it was specially adapted to the minds of the islanders; who are susceptible to no impressions, except from things palpable, or novel and striking. To them a dry sermon would be dry indeed.[20]

Melville also described the Catholic chapel at Papeete. It was made of bamboo, was quite small, and was surmounted by a cross. The altar had a crucifix, gilded candlesticks, and censers. The natives thought that "masses and chants were nothing more than evil spells. "As for the priests themselves, they were no better than diabolical sorcerers; like those who, in old times, terrified their fathers."[21]

Melville described the priests' living quarters as quite sumptuous for the South Seas. As for the priests, themselves, "they were little, dried-up Frenchmen, in long, straight gowns of black cloth, and unsightly three-cornered hats, so preposterously big, that, in putting them on, the reverend fathers seemingly extinguished themselves."[22] One of the priests turned out to be an Irishman, Father Murphy, who had studied for the priesthood in France. He took a liking to several of the sailors who were also Irish. One day, three of the French priests came to pay a visit to the sailors. Melville wrote that "English missionaries were leaving their cards for us in the shape of a package of tracts, we could not help thinking, that the Frenchmen, in making a personal call, were at least much better bred."[23]

One can see in these descriptions that Herman Melville was not very impressed with the Catholic missionaries. He believed that they were inept, to say the least. In fact, he perceived both the Protestant and Catholic missionaries to be inept and out of place in this South Seas paradise.

The Tahitians can hardly ever be said to reflect; they are all impulse; and so, instead of expounding dogmas, the missionaries give them the large type, pleasing cuts, and short and easy lessons of the primer. Hence, anything like a permanent religious impression is seldom or never produced.[24]

Melville believed that the very traits of the Tahitians which persuaded the London Missionary Society to regard them as most promising subjects for conversion proved to be the greatest obstruction to that conversion. The natives had "an air of softness in their manners, great apparent ingenuousness and docility." But

these were the mere accompaniments of an indolence, bodily and mental; a constitutional voluptuousness; and an aversion to the least restraint; which, however fitted for the luxurious state of nature, in the tropics, are the greatest possible hindrances to the strict moralities of Christianity.[25]

After several months, Melville grew tired of beachcombing and observing the Tahitians, and wished to extend his travels. He decided to look for another whaler in need of able-bodied men. He found the *Charles & Henry*, out of Nantucket, at Eimeo and, on 4 November 1842, Melville signed the ship's articles. He did not want to part from Long Ghost, but Captain Coleman was suspicious of the doctor, and Long Ghost remained behind in Tahiti.

The *Charles & Henry* departed Tahiti to look for whales in the seas around Japan. But whaling off Japan was poor, and the *Charles & Henry* put in at Lahaina, Maui, in the Hawaiian Islands, on 27 April 1843. To Melville's terror, a week later, the *Acushnet*, from which he had originally deserted, pulled into Lahaina. Melville knew he risked arrest, as the captain had filed charges against the sailors who had deserted. Melville barely escaped arrest by cleverly avoiding meeting the crew until the *Acushnet* sailed for the Japanese whaling grounds; when it had safely sailed off, he had a couple of days to explore Maui before his ship sailed on to Honolulu. In Honolulu, Melville was officially discharged on 4 May according to the agreement he had made in Tahiti.

The Hawaiian, or Sandwich, Islands (named by Captain Cooke for the Earl of Sandwich) had been first discovered by Captain James Cooke, the great English navigator who had landed on the island of Kauai on 14 February 1779. Kamehameha I came to the throne of Oahu in 1782 and, as a strong leader, succeeded in conquering all of the islands except Kauai and Niihau, which shortly volunteered to become part of the federation. During this period, Kamehameha developed the sandalwood trade with the western world, the wood being much prized for its lovely aroma. Kamehameha treated foreigners well, but he was strict about the European's vices, such as alcoholism, rape, and crime; he maintained law and order, and demanded the destruction of all distilleries. Kamehameha was interested in the foreigners' teachings, however, and sought to obtain Christian teachers. But having been unsuccessful in these pre-missionary times, he ordered a strict observance of the native Hawaiian religion. Foreign influences nevertheless undermined the old religious system. In 1804, an epidemic, probably cholera, destroyed a great part of the population. The last human sacrifices were performed in 1807.

Kamehameha I got his wish for Christian teachers in 1820, shortly after his death. The next period of Hawaiian history began with the arrival of the first company of missionaries from New England in this year. During the next thirty-five years, fourteen other missionary companies followed. These included more than one hundred fifty men and women of a variety of skills and training: ministers, teachers, physicians, printers, farmers, and businessmen. The New Englanders introduced the Congregational Church to the natives, started schools, and began a printing industry.

The Hawaiians were most eager to learn. As the missionaries learned the language, they translated it into written form by transliterating the sounds into the English alphabet, and printed textbooks. The churches were well attended, and Christianity soon came to be regarded as the national religion.

Interest in the adoption of this New England Christianity as a personal religion culminated in what was termed the Great Revival in 1823, when Queen Keopuolani, Kamehameha I's wife and the mother of the next two kings, Kamehameha II and Kamehameha III, became the first convert. Many chiefs also joined the church at this time.

These missionaries from Boston and other New England towns represented the conservative elements of Protestant Christianity: they brought their Calvinistic doctrines of behavior and salvation with them. Interestingly, it was mostly the other whites living in the islands who opposed the strengthening of this missionary movement. The British, French, and United-States consuls also opposed the growing power of the missionaries. Moreover, there was trouble over the Catholic priests who came in 1827, and who were banished in 1831 on the grounds that they were reviving idolatry, which had been outlawed since 1819. The Catholics, however, returned and began the building of their cathedral in 1840. From that date forward, they expanded their membership rapidly. Next came the Mormon missionaries in 1850, whose church grew to a large membership and built a magnificent temple on Oahu.

As seemed to be his fate, Herman Melville arrived in Honolulu on the island of Oahu during a political crisis. Lord George Paulett had seized the Sandwich Islands in the name of Queen Victoria in the previous February (1843). The missionary advisors to Kamehameha had advised the king to seek annexation to the United States, as they feared the French insurgence in the South Seas. King Kamehameha III had sent a plea to President Tyler to intercede and to return his independent status. But the United States Senate was not in favor of the annexation at this time, and the British took up the slack. Eventually, the British Admiral returned the island's sovereignty. The territories were finally annexed by the United States in 1898 by a joint resolution of Congress, made a territory in 1900, and the fiftieth state of the Union in 1959.

In Honolulu, Melville found that the missionaries had literally taken over control of King Kamehameha III and of almost everything on the island. The people had lost their native arts, and the population had declined precipitously since the missionaries had arrived. In the end, Melville concluded that Christianity had brought the Sandwich Islands only slavery: he believed that the islanders were now degraded persons. In *Omoo*, Melville ridicules the missionaries' apparent success in gaining religious conversion among the natives of the Hawaiian Islands:

> In fact, there is, perhaps, no race upon earth less disposed by nature to the monitions of Christianity than the people of the South Seas. And this assertion is made with full knowledge of what is called the 'Great Revival at the Sandwich Islands,' about the year 1836; when several thousand were, in the course of a few weeks, admitted to the bosom of the Church. But this result was brought about by no sober moral convictions; as an almost instantaneous relapse into every kind of licentiousness soon afterwards testified. It was the legitimate effect of a morbid feeling, engendered by the sense of severe physical wants, preying upon minds excessively prone to superstition; and by fanatical preaching, inflamed into the belief, that the gods of the missionaries were taking vengeance upon the wickedness of the land.[26]

It is this aspect of Melville's South Seas adventures, and his two literary efforts based on them, upon which we must concentrate, for this was Melville's first personal great awakening and disillusionment concerning organized religion. The fortuitous "puberty rites" which life itself had bestowed upon the boy Melville surely raised serious questions about the Calvinistic doctrines upon which he had been raised, but these pertained to Calvinism (and Unitarianism) against a backdrop of accustomed artifices of Western civilization. The effect was thus dimmed and ambiguous. The stark contrast presented to Melville by the natural and innocent human lifestyle of the South Seas natives vis-à-vis the supernatural contrivances of Western religion, however, offered Melville startling insights. It was meeting the missionaries and seeing what they were doing to the natives that turned his mind against proselytizing in the name of the Christian religion, and set his mind to questioning the very content of Christianity.

It was while he was in the Marquesas, and later on other islands in the South Seas—notably in the Hawaiian Islands—that Melville had observed the missionaries, Protestant and Catholic, who had come to save the natives from Hell. Melville believed that the peoples of the South Seas involved themselves in little reflection, and acted primarily upon impulse. This gave the missionaries, Protestant and Catholic alike, little opportunity to teach the natives their own respective brands of Christian dogma, as the natives would scarcely have understood them any more than the Indians in Reverend John Eliot's town of Natick in 1651 could understand the intricacies of the theology of Calvinism which Eliot believed. The missionaries in the South Seas, therefore, tried to suppress the natives' apparent worship of idols, to curb what was the Polynesians' natural sexual freedom, to cover up their nakedness, and to do away with some of their more exotic dancing. Toward this end, the missionaries hired some of the natives to act as constables snooping in the groves in the evening and poking around the native huts to find amorous couples. The offenders were then sentenced to do some road work on the island.

But the lack of regard for the native customs and the implicit assumption of the missionaries that they would save the natives from the fires of Hell made Melville realize that the missionaries were really out of place in this kind of a culture. He was especially struck by the missionaries' motives in the Hawaiian Islands, where they not only took over the minds of the natives, but also most of their property.

Melville is not as critical of the missionaries in *Omoo*, but some of Melville's observations of the Hawaiian missionaries' activities give us some insights as to what he thought of the missionaries' activities in Tahiti.

cf Nor has such an opportunity for a display of missionary rhetoric been allowed to pass by unimproved! But when these philanthropists send us such glowing accounts one-half of their labors, why does their modesty restrain them from publishing the other half of the good they have wrought? Not until I visited Honolulu was I aware of the fact that the small remnant of the natives had been civilized into draft horses, and evangelized into beasts of
NB. burden. But so it is. They have literally been broken into the traces, and are harnessed to the vehicles of their spiritual instructors like so many dumb brutes.[27]

In *Typee*, Melville is candid; the book was Melville's first, and represented the young man's discovery with respect to the natural life of the native tribes, as contrasted with what passed for civilization in the West. He pulled no punches in pointing out what to him seemed absurdly obvious now, and scorned the civilization that the missionaries had brought to the people of the South Seas. He asked if the natives were happier and better off after a quarter of a century of proselytizing:

cf Let the once smiling and populous Hawaiian Islands, with their now diseased, starving, and dying natives, answer the question. The missionaries may seek to disguise the matter as they will, but the facts are incontrovertible; and the most devout Christian who visits that group with an unbiased mind, must go away mournfully asking, "Are these, alas! the fruits of twenty-five years of enlightening?"[28] NB

To contrast further the civilization of the Western nations with that of the South Seas natives, Melville used the odious notion of cannibalism, pointing out that only on sporadic occasions did they practice this art; "they are such only when they seek to gratify the passion of revenge upon their enemies." Then he asked

cf whether the mere eating of human flesh so very far exceeds in barbarity that custom which only a few years since was practiced in enlightened England: a convicted traitor, perhaps a man found guilty of honesty, patriotism, and suchlike heinous crimes, had his head lopped off with a huge ax, his bowels dragged out and thrown into a fire; while his body carved into four quarters, was with his head exposed upon pikes, and permitted to rot and fester among the public haunts of men![29]

Melville enlarged upon man's cruelty to man in the so-called enlightened and Christian cultures by writing,

The fiend-like skill we display in the invention of all manner of death-dealing weapons, the vindictiveness with which we carry on our wars, and the misery and desolation that follows in their train, are enough of themselves to distinguish the white civilized man as the most ferocious animal on the face of the earth.[30]

It is needless to multiply the examples of civilized barbarity; they far exceed in the amount of misery they cause the crimes which we regard with such abhorrence in our less enlightened fellow creatures.[31]

It was passages such as these that, after the book's publication, invoked no small amount of pressure to censor some of the words of the author. Those people in London and Boston who were sacrificing, they thought, to bring the South Seas Islanders to Christ and to save their souls, didn't want to read these words from a traveler who had visited the islands and had become acquainted with the missionary movement. There was a lot of criticism from those with a vested interest in the missionary movement. For Melville, this criticism simply made him more disillusioned about organized Christian religion.

Melville knew that he would be attacked by those who believed in the missions. His response was that

those things which I have stated as facts will remain facts, in spite of whatever the bigoted or incredulous may say or write against them. My reflections, however, on those facts may not be free from error. If such be the case I claim no further indulgence than should be conceded to every man whose object is to do good.[32]

There can be no doubt that not all of what Melville perceived was caused directly by the missionaries but also in his mind. Melville, like most other Westerners, equated Western culture with Christianity, largely because Westerners have always generally believed that their culture is Christian.

From this, it is clear that Melville was not opposed to civilization itself, nor to Christianity, nor even to missionaries; in fact, he believed in them.

> Lest the slightest misconception should arise from anything thrown out in this chapter or indeed in any other part of the volume, let me here observe, that against the cause of missions in the abstract no Christian can possibly be opposed; it is in truth a just and holy cause.[33]

Melville's complaint was that what the missionaries were accomplishing was the antithesis of true Christian spirituality.

> But if the great end proposed by it be spiritual, the agency employed to accomplish that end is purely earthly; and although the object in view be the achievement of much good, that agency may nevertheless be productive of evil. In short, missionary undertaking, however it may be blessed of Heaven, is in itself but human; and subject, like everything else, to errors and abuses. And have not errors and abuses crept into the most sacred places, and may there not be unworthy or incapable missionaries abroad, as well as ecclesiastics of a similar character at home? May not the unworthiness of incapacity of those who assume apostolic functions upon the remote islands of the sea more easily escape detection by the world at large than if it were displayed in the heart of a city?[34]

In fairness to the missionaries, Melville blamed civilization itself.

> In justice to the missionaries, however, I will willingly admit, that whatever evils may have resulted from their collective mismanagement of the business of the mission, and from the want of vital piety evinced by some of their number, still the present deplorable conditions of the Sandwich Islands is by no means wholly chargeable to them. . . . In a word, here, as in every case where Civilization has in any way been introduced among those whom we call savages, she has scattered her vices, and withheld her blessings.[35]

ck. Thus, we have seen that Melville not only reacted against the Calvinism and determinism of the Dutch Reformed Church in which he was reared, but also that his contacts with Liverpool, England, and with Christian missionaries in the South Seas further disillusioned him as to Western civilization as a whole. He did not blame Christianity as an abstract ideal, and he knew that it would be unfair to blame all of the sordid conditions of the people of the South Seas on the missionaries. But Melville realized, as many have since, that Western Christian civilization, so-called, had brought disaster to these pristinely perfect natural people.

In the duration of about four months in Honolulu, Melville had held several odd jobs: a pin boy in a bowling alley, a clerk, and bookkeeper. But his life would take on a drastic change when the frigate *United States* of the United States Navy arrived in Honolulu on 3 August 1843. Two weeks later, on 17 August, Melville's name was added to the muster roll of the *United States*. It was to take the frigate almost eighteen months to get back to Boston, spending a good deal of time on the west coast of South America. But we shall deal with this voyage when we discuss Melville's humanism for on board ship he witnessed cruelties which strongly reinforced his view of how men should treat one another.

CHAPTER THREE
MELVILLE AND SOCIAL IDEALISM

The easiest way for Herman Melville to get back home from Honolulu was to enlist in the United States Navy. On 17 August 1843, Melville signed on to the U.S. Navy frigate the *United States*, which was slated to return to the Boston navy yard. Herman's name was added to the ship's muster roll as an ordinary seaman, his contract being for three years or the length of the cruise, whichever was shorter. Despite his experience with the terrible conditions of shipboard life on a whaler, Melville was unprepared for what he would encounter over the next year and a half.

He was particularly shaken when, the very day after leaving Honolulu, the captain summoned all of the crew on the deck to witness the flogging of several men for drunkenness and other shore leave misdemeanors. Although shore leave could be expected to produce such behavior among sailors, it was insisted coldly that navy discipline had to be maintained. As Melville describes the summons,

> [The crew] were startled by the dread summons of the boatswain and his mates at the principal hatchway—a summons that ever sends a shudder through every manly heart in a frigate: *All hands witness punishment, ahoy!*[1]

Melville wanted to absent himself from what was to ensue, but regulations enjoined "the attendance of the entire ship's company, from the corpulent captain himself to the smallest boy who strikes the bell."[2] Everyone having gathered on deck, the Captain came forward from his cabin. "Master-at-arms, bring up the prisoners," he said. When the four men had been brought up from the brig, the Captain routinely asked them if they had anything to say about their fighting the day before. But there really was no defense; no one would admit that he had struck the first blow.

The prisoners were prepared for the flogging: the men removed their jackets and shirts which were loosely thrown over their shoulders. Then,

> at a sign from the Captain, John, with a shameless leer, advanced and stood passively upon the grating, while the bare-headed old quarter-master, with gray hair streaming in the wind, bound his feet to the cross-bars, and, stretching out his arms over his head, secured them to the hammock netting above. He then retreated a little space, standing silent. . . .
>
> The Captain's finger was now lifted, and the first boatswain's-mate, combing out the nine tails of his *cat* with his hand, and then sweeping them around his neck, brought them with the whole force of his body upon the mark. Again, and again, and again; and at every blow, higher and higher rose the long, purple bars on the prisoner's back. But he only bowed over his head, and stood still . . . One dozen lashes being applied, the man was taken down, and went among the crew with a smile, saying, "D—n me! It's nothing when you're used to it! Who wants to fight."[3]

After docking at several harbors on the west coast of Central and South America, the *United States*, having rounded Cape Horn, finally arrived in Boston Harbor on 3 October 1844. It had been nearly four years since Melville had left New Bedford for the whaling grounds of the Pacific aboard the *Acushnet*. Now, it took another ten days to clear the ship; the crew was paid off and Melville was discharged. Herman caught a steamboat for New York where he met his brother Gansevoort who had just been campaigning for a presidential candidate named James K. Polk.

Herman was now twenty-five, a young man barely across the threshold of adulthood, yet with a head full of mind-boggling experiences. But Melville himself did not yet realize how much genuine education these past four years had given him. As Melville himself somewhat mistakenly later wrote in a letter to Nathaniel Hawthorne, "Until I was twenty-five, I had no development at all. From my twenty-fifth year I date my life. Three weeks have scarcely passed, at any time between then and now that I have not unfolded within myself."[4]

When Herman Melville arrived home in Lansingburgh, he found that family conditions were still difficult. Gansevoort had been hoping that Polk would be elected and would appoint him to a good-paying political job, but the family was still largely dependent upon its maternal relatives. Fortunately for the Melvilles, James Polk did win the Presidency in the national election of that year (1844), and he did reward Herman's older brother for his campaign efforts. On 16 July 1845, Gansevoort was appointed Secretary of the Legation of the United States of America in London.

Herman's family and friends encouraged him to recount his South Seas experiences. Melville was almost too willing, and reeled off yarn after entertaining yarn about the sea, the whaling industry, and the South Seas islands. Since books about travel in unknown and exotic parts of the world were popular in the middle of the nineteenth century, someone suggested that Herman might write about his experiences for financial gain. Melville set immediately to the task.

Over the winter of 1844-1845, Herman Melville completed his manuscript, which he entitled *Typee*, and sent it off to Harper and Brothers in New York City. The first reader for the publishing house, a Mr. Saunders, praised the work and compared it to *Robinson Crusoe*, a very popular and best-selling book at that time, but Harper and Brothers concluded that "it was impossible that it could be true and therefore was without real value."[5]

Gansevoort, who was off to London on his diplomatic assignment at this time, took the manuscript with him and showed it to John Murray, a leading English publisher. Murray, too, was somewhat suspicious of the authenticity of the narrative, but was interested enough in the book to pay one hundred pounds for the privilege of printing in England a first edition of one thousand copies. Because of the poor copyright laws then in effect, it was necessary also to publish the book simultaneously in the United States, and in January 1846, Wiley and Putnam was persuaded to publish the United States edition. The bound volume was issued in both countries the next month, the American edition was called simply *Typee*, while the English edition bore the weighty title, *Narrative of a Four Month's Residence Among the Natives of a Valley of the Marquesas Islands*.

Significantly, Herman Melville had dedicated the book to Lemuel Shaw, Chief Justice of the Commonwealth of Massachusetts, whose family had been lifelong friends of the Melvill(e) family. On 19 March 1846, Herman was able to send the first copy of the book to Judge Shaw. It should be noted for our purposes that the Lemuel Shaws were prominent Boston Unitarians. While Unitarianism was still a controversial version of Christianity, it had achieved denominational status in 1825 with the founding of the American Unitarian Association headquartered in Boston, and a great many New Englanders, as well as groups elsewhere in the United States, were publicly professed Unitarians.

Typee was generally well received in the United States. Margaret Fuller, the New England Transcendentalist, reviewed the book for the *New York Daily Tribune* calling it "a very entertaining and pleasing narrative."[6] George Ripley also reviewed it in *The Harbinger* and compared it with Charles Henry Dana's *Two Years Before the Mast*.[7]

Except for the weighty criticism which emanated from the missionary societies, the English edition also was well received, but the missionaries and related vested interests brought so much pressure that in the second edition, some of the offensive passages were deleted. This new edition was reviewed in the *Biblical Repository and Classical Review* for October 1849.

> We are glad to see that the good sense of the author has induced, and the moral sentiments of the world constrained him, in revising his work, to strike out those parts which related to mission-

ary operations in Tahiti and the Sandwich Islands, which contained assertions reckless and charges gratuitous and false.[8]

A review in *The Friend*, a Honolulu journal, was typical of some of the criticism of the vested missionary interests:

> If the author had erased other passages, we think he would have shown good judgment . . . Such course would certainly have led him to suppress some of those glaring facts respecting his habits of gross and shameless familiarity not to say unblushing licentiousness with a tribe of debased and filthy savages of the Marquesas . . . sunk lower than the debased people.[9]

An article possibly written by Charles F. Briggs on "Honolulu" appeared in *Holden's Dollar Magazine* in which the author noted that Melville's account of the Christian missionaries in *Omoo* which had been claimed to be "grossly exaggerated, or wholly untrue." But, he added,

> We should hope, for the honor of our missionaries, that Mr. Melville's sketches were made from hearsay, rather than actual observation, for he represents a condition of society which would be disgraceful to any civilized being, much less the heralds of the cross who have been sent abroad to preach the Gospel of Christ to the nations that sit in darkness.[10]

Not only did Melville not believe that these people "sat in darkness," he believed that Western civilization promoted by the missionaries had only brought misery rather than any light or hope. When *Typee* was reviewed in *The United States Catholic Magazine and Monthly Review*, the reviewer made certain that his readers understood about the religion of the author of the book, for he wrote, "The author is a Protestant."[11]

An article on "Polynesia" in *The English Review* commented on *Typee* and *Omoo*, stating,

> there is . . . a laxity of moral feeling, an absence of religious principle . . . and the jesting tone, or the inoffensive expression which accompany or veil the most objectionable passages, make them yet more pernicious. In *Typee*, these things are less apparent, though that work is deserving of severe censure. In *Omoo*, how-

ever, the cloven foot is much too visible to be mistaken, despite the common place declarations of respect for religion and morals.[12]

With characteristic bad luck for the Melville family, Gansevoort became gravely ill shortly after the publication of *Typee*'s first edition. He died in London on 12 May 1846. (The next day, President Polk proclaimed that a state of war existed between the United States and Mexico.) Gansevoort Melville had been the financial mainstay of the family. Now, not only was he (and his income) gone, Gansevoort's illness itself had been a serious financial drain. Now the head of the family, Herman, wrote to President Polk to ask the United States government to pay for the funeral expenses and for shipping the body back to the United States. On 6 June, President Polk authorized the Ambassador in London, Louis McLane, to pay for the funeral expenses of Gansevoort Melville.

With new family responsibilities, Herman threw his energies into writing a sequel to *Typee*. In this work, he was careful to mitigate his outrage at what civilization was doing to the native tribes of the South Seas. An important goal of this new literary effort was to bring in money and, since the public had so responded to the tales of unfamiliar places and peoples of the South Seas, Herman aimed to capitalize on this aspect. He early entitled the new work *Omoo*, to the delight of modern crossword-puzzle fans. As previously mentioned, the word *omoo* means wanderer in Polynesian. This book, published in April 1847, by Harper and Brothers, was also a great success.

Perhaps this was the happiest year of Melville's life since his childhood, for now he was an acknowledged author and, that same year, he became engaged to marry Judge Shaw's daughter Elizabeth. Elizabeth, a close friend of Herman's sisters, was a good Boston girl, and certainly bore little, if any, resemblance to Fayaway, the Polynesian romantic figure in *Typee*. Their marriage took place on 4 August 1847, the ceremony performed by Reverend Dr. Alexander Young, minister of the New Old South Church (Unitarian) in Boston.[13] Before the wedding, Elizabeth had received communion from Reverend James Freeman Clarke, a renowned Boston Unitarian minister.[14] Judge Shaw gave Herman and Elizabeth three thousand dollars with which to begin their married life. They honeymooned for three weeks in New Hampshire and Quebec, before returning to Lansingburgh.

Just one month later, Herman's brother Allan was married to Sophia Eliza Thurston. The two couples decided to relocate in New York City and pooled their resources to buy a house at 103 Fourth Avenue. It may have been largely Herman's royalties and Judge Shaw's wedding gift which made this possible; supplementally, Melville borrowed an additional two thousand dollars from his new father-in-law. The decision to buy one house between them may have been made on the idea that *three* families could, in effect, live as cheaply as one, for, not only the two newlywed couples, but also the Melville mother, the four unmarried sisters, and the youngest brother, Thomas, followed along to the new residence. By 1950, the joint household, including four domestics and two infants, totaled no fewer than sixteen residents. Malcolm was born to Herman and Elizabeth, and Maria Gansevoort to Allan and Sophia, in mid-February 1849, just two days apart. Malcolm was christened at the Melville home by the Reverend Henry Whitney Bellows, now the young new minister of the First Unitarian Church which, the reader will recall, had gotten its start around the corner from where Herman Melville had been born that very same year.

It is interesting to note that the Melville family's new home at 103 Fourth Avenue was also not far from the second building occupied by the now prosperous First Congregational Church of New York City. The cornerstone for the church's first meeting house had been laid on 29 April 1820 at Chambers Street, between Broadway and Church Streets, and the completed building had been dedicated on 20 January 1821. The Reverend Edward Everett, a young man who was shortly to distinguish himself as an orator, statesman, and president of Harvard College, had delivered the dedicatory sermon.[15] The society had called William Ware (the brother of Henry Ware, Jr.) to be the first minister. A little over twenty years later, a large chunk of cornice fell from the ceiling almost at the spot where Reverend Henry Whitney Bellows, who had been installed in 1839, was standing. That accident had persuaded a reluctant congregation to seek the new building site on Broadway, between Prince and Spring Streets.

The new church building was designed by Minard Lefever, a prominent architect at that time; yet the construction of the new edifice was a comedy of errors, the result of which was that the side walls had to be propped up to sustain the weight of the roof. It was a large edifice which could seat over twelve hundred people. The building was named the Church of the Divine Unity, although the congregation legally remained the First Congregational Church of New York City. George Templeton Strong, a prominent lawyer who kept a diary, characterized the new church: "There's the new Unitarian meeting house on Crosby Street show front on Broadway—Gothic in the Chinese style, and a more deplorable example of infatuated vulgarity trying to look venerable and medieval."[16] Mr. Strong had strong opinions, and he was no friend of the Unitarians, although a good friend of Bellows.

This is, of course, the church in which the newlywed Herman Melvilles rented their first pew sometime after they had settled into their new house, and had adjusted to what we might imagine to have been something of a cacophonic family life for newlyweds living in such a large household. Although there are no pew-rental records of the Melvilles before 1849, we must presume that the Melvilles first merely attended, and later rented a pew. The earliest records show that, for $14.30, they rented pew number 117, which was assessed at two hundred dollars, for the second half of 1849 (which they paid in 1850). This is probably the first time the Herman Melvilles had funds enough to afford the luxury of their own pew, albeit only a rented one. Allan was just starting out on an new career as a lawyer; Herman was only barely launched in his career as an author. In addition to their wives and newborn offspring, both brothers had to support their mother, sisters, and brother Thomas, not to mention the servants. Herman had exhausted his receipts from *Typee* and *Omoo*, and had yet to repay his father-in-law the loan of two thousand dollars. What he had hoped to be a masterpiece (*Mardi*, published earlier in 1849) had been a dismal failure. His next significant income was only beginning to generate with the success of *Redburn*, which was published in September of 1850.

As a proper New York family, Herman and Elizabeth attended church, and may have chosen The Church of the Divine Unity solely because Mrs. Melville was from an Unitarian background. But this seems insufficient a reason, especially as Herman's mother and her daughters were now avowedly in the Dutch Reformed Church and attended services at one of the many fine old New York Dutch ecclesiastical edifices. Allan and Sophia seem to have attended an Episcopal church. Herman had long ago declined his mother's example of becoming Calvinist and, considering his disillusionment with orthodox Christian missionaries, it is more likely that he actually *preferred* Reverend Bellows' sermons to any available alternatives.

We have already seen that Herman Melville was rather intensely interested in religion. His faithful recalling and describing of chapels and churches in the various islands as well as on shipboard give us a clue to this, and his relating about ministers, priests, and missionaries, even to the details of their clothing as well as to their sermon content (or lack thereof), comprise further evidence that religious questions were beginning to intensify in Melville's awareness. At this stage in his life, however, I think that we could say only that Herman Melville was *interested* in religion, not that he himself was religious.

Church service attendance was still a family institution in America, but the Melville clan at Fourth Avenue felt free to choose disparate denominations.[17] We may imagine (with some amusement) no fewer than ten people pouring out of the home at church time on a Sunday morning, and then parting to attend different services.

Herman Melville now ambitiously focused upon the career that fate seemed to have chosen for him, but he had had very little formal education. Already well-read by the time he had sailed for Liverpool, Herman had nevertheless been forced to abandon school in his adolescent years, and additional years of sailing adventures had deprived him of opportunities for any serious reading or intellectual study. Melville later remarked that the decks of a whaler had been his Harvard and Yale. In the words of Leon Howard, "Melville drew his material from his experiences, from his imagination, and from a variety of travel books when the memory of his experiences failed him or when his personal observations were inadequate."[18]

But an important part of any writer's job is to read, and one of the advantages of living in New York City was the availability of libraries which Melville now used liberally. He read everything that he could lay his hands upon, especially about the South Seas. Milton Sealts devoted an entire book to the subject of Herman Melville's avid taste for books, and to the specific titles which he can document that Melville read. Sealts lists some of the variety and breadth of Melville's interests:

Since the late 1930s, a succession of enlightening articles and monographs has demonstrated the stimulus of books—the Bible, the literature of travel, the prose of Sealts, page cadences of Sir Thomas Browne, the poetry of Shakespeare and Milton, the thought of Plato and Bayle—in releasing [Melville's] creative energies.[19]

Further into this book, Dr. Sealts points out that

while in Boston Melville, of course, had access to the private library of his father-in-law, Lemuel Shaw, which was by no means limited to legal subjects. Judge Shaw subscribed to such journals as the *North American Review* (to which he contributed), the *Christian Register* (the Unitarian journal).[20]

F. O. Matheissen stresses that Herman Melville's reading profoundly influenced his own life and thought, saying, "The books that really spoke to Melville became an immediate part of him to a degree hardly matched by any other of our great writers in their maturity."[21]

Melville's success with *Typee* and *Omoo* entitled him entry into the most famous literary clique in the city. Melville became a member of the New York Society Library (which, as synchronicity would have it, is now located on East Seventy-ninth Street, near the All Souls Church, the *fourth* building of the city's first Unitarian society). Melville moved in the social circles of the intelligentsia of the city, socializing with William Cullen Bryant (a member of All Souls Church), the Duyckincks, and other prominent thinkers.[22] Evert Augustus Duyckinck and his younger brother, George Long Duyckinck, were particularly outstanding members of the New York literary and publishing world. Evert was the son of a publisher and was the editor of Wiley and Putnam's *Library of Choice Reading*. He also initiated several literary magazines. Melville was a particularly avid borrower from Evert Duyckinck's rather extensive library. Evert and Melville became fast friends until the former's death in 1878. When Melville was not contacting Evert, he was writing or meeting with his younger brother George.

The material poverty of Melville's adolescence and the particularly stressful ardor of sea life were finally giving way to a promise of the prosperous and prestigious life for the young man. His career now seemed to have been chosen for him; he would become—indeed, already was—a writer, and, far from the stereotypic chilly bohemian garret associated with followers of the Muses, Melville was now enjoying a choice spot in the fashionable New York literary limelight. Nevertheless, the hearth of home may not have been as comfortable and comforting as the elect group of literary elite of the New York Society Library with whom Herman was keeping company. "The joint household on Fourth Avenue being a crowded one, the New York Society Library rooms may well have provided the young author with a welcome retreat. as work on *Mardi* continued."[23] From what Melville later wrote in *Pierre* about his mother, one doubts that all of this variegated family living together under one roof was a happy arrangement.

All of this was happening so fully and rapidly that it is hardly a wonder that Melville did not appreciate the educational value of his sea experiences at this time. But they were processing within the hidden recesses of his mind, nevertheless. The recounting of his sea adventures to friends and relatives when Melville had returned from Honolulu, and especially his writing of them, had helped Herman to accommodate not only these diverse and multifarious experiences, but also those of his childhood and traumatic adolescence. An integrated perspective on life was beginning to take on some form, even if still embryonic, now in his late twenties. His reading was almost placental to this embryo, nurturing and nourishing his personal perspective, and carrying off the wastes. In reading and in writing his own manuscripts, Herman found himself thinking more and more seriously about some of the things through which he had lived before he was twenty-five. The Liverpool experience came back again and again to him. The depths of meaning from his whaling experiences and his experiences on the *United States* began to surface above the threshold of his consciousness. The questions, perhaps only implicit before, about his family's trials and tribulations also began to take on more definitive shape.

That personal stirrings of a genuinely religious sort were also gestating in the womb of Melville's subconscious can be glimpsed in his third novel, *Mardi*, which he had set about writing early in 1848, and which was published in the spring of that year. It was this effort which, though devastatingly unsuccessful, would lay the foundations for his later masterpieces, Moby-Dick and *Billy Budd.* Indeed, in *Mardi*, Melville displays the themes that were most weighing on his mind; the messages he wanted to work through to full clarity for himself, and to disseminate to the reading public. *Mardi* also displays the central literary device through which he would explore these issues—not just the form of the novel but, in particular, allegory. Because these themes and the form of allegory were still immature in the young writer, and because

Mardi deserves special focus, the work will be discussed in the next chapter.

In the meantime, a humanistic rather than religious perspective had matured in Melville, a perspective which poured out with convincing eloquence in Melville's next two efforts, *Redburn* and *White-Jacket*. The trip to Liverpool had awakened the social conscience of Herman Melville; it was given new grist from his experiences in the South Seas, and new depth on the U.S. Navy ship. Although Melville continued to raise the questions that he had raised so poorly in *Mardi*—the philosophical and metaphysical questions lying at the root of human indifference to human suffering and sorrow—he was always faced with dichotomy between the ideal of how human life could and should be, and the contradictions in how the Western world actually implemented its own espoused values.

In *Redburn*, Melville drew upon his experiences in sailing to Liverpool in 1839. By now he was learning what would ire the critics and the reading public; thus, lest he fail to recapture his reputation as a new and promising author, Melville wrote the tale in entertaining and adventurous form. Somewhat cynically, he described *Redburn* and *White-Jacket* to his father-in-law as two *jobs*, which he had done for money—being forced to it, as other men are to sawing wood.

And, indeed, Melville turned out two books, each of which got good reviews. But it seems clear from his eloquent outcries that he was hoping to awaken his public's social conscience as the experience had awakened his own. Describing the literally starving mother and children in particularly graphic and heart-wrenching lucidity, Melville hoped his readers, too, would stand where he had once stood, and feel the same sensations of horror.

> I stood looking down at them, while my whole soul swelled within me; and I asked myself, What right had any body in this wide world to smile and be glad, when sights like this were to be seen? It was enough to turn the heart to gall . . . For who were these ghosts that I saw. Were they not human beings? A woman and two girls? With eyes, and lips, and

ears like any queen? With hearts which, though they did not bound with blood, yet beat with a dull, dead ache that was their life.[24]

In Liverpool, Melville had found not only starvation and poverty, he had also found a repugnant indifference of others to the sad conditions, which probably shocked him even more than the outrageous suffering.

Redburn is full of such vivid and starkly contrasting descriptions of the suffering on the one hand and the social indifference to it on the other. But in *Redburn*, Melville also focused in on the Industrial Revolution and its so-called successful results. Later in his life, he was to write several short stories which further sharpened the reader's mind as to the effects of this Industrial Revolution on people. "The Tartarus of Maids" is the best example, for this story is set in an isolated New England paper mill town; the young factory girls live in mill-owned dormitories built for this purpose, living and working virtually around the clock in the white-paper environment, the girls end up *looking* like paper, with their sallow complexions and other properties more typical of paper than of human beings.

One of Melville's best known short stories is "Bartleby the Scrivener" which illustrates another side of this same Industrial Revolution, for Bartelby is the copier of law briefs in a law office who more and more withdraws within himself until he ceases to be a person, and to be alive.

Herman Melville was not the only thinking person to question the results of the Industrial Revolution. Some of the New England Transcendentalists, such as Henry David Thoreau, also were vividly aware of what this material success was doing to the human soul. *Walden* is essentially a protest about the results of the Industrial Revolution, to which his antidote is nature. A more natural human life was also the recommended antidote of Ralph Waldo Emerson in his Divinity School Address of 1838. In this address, Emerson told his listeners that the institutions of this world were not so important as individual return to nature. This return to nature crops up often in Western culture; the hippie culture of the 1960s, for example, represents but one manifestation of this movement in modern times.

Redburn was published in September 1849 by Bentley in London, while Harpers published the first American edition. Melville himself journeyed to London on 11 October to arrange for the novel's publication. He sailed for New York on Christmas Day of 1849. This new book was written in the style which had originally brought Melville acclaim. In *Holden's Dollar Magazine*, Charles F. Briggs commented that "the descriptions of Liverpool are . . . the best part of the book; he notices precisely those objects that must first strike the eye of a sailor boy on arriving at that port."[25]

But we may perceive from such reviews that Americans had missed the point of Melville's efforts, and bought the books merely because they were so entertaining. This surely must have had the effect of dividing Melville's own soul, part bedazzled by prestige and gold; part struggling to work out the deepest meanings of life. Melville immediately threw himself into writing *White-Jacket*, a story set on board a man-of-war ship, revealing another view of Melville's social consciousness, the semi-autobiographical story of his year and a half aboard the *United States*, a navy frigate. The name of the fictional counterpart of the *United States* is *Neversink*. Referring to the flogging scenes he had so painfully witnessed ten years earlier, the point that Melville makes is unmistakable.

Let us have the charity to believe them, as we do, when some Captains in the Navy say, that the thing of all others most repulsive to them, in the routine of what they consider their duty, is the administration of corporal punishment upon the crew; for surely, not to feel scarified to the quick at these scenes would argue a man but a beast. You see a human being, stripped like a slave, scourged worse than a hound. And for what? For things not essentially criminal, but only made so by arbitrary laws.[26]

Melville devotes four chapters to descriptions and criticism of flogging; if this isn't clear enough, Melville then devotes an entire chapter explicitly to "Some of the Evil Effects of Flogging," in which he presents the navy's arguments for corporal punishment—chiefly, that it consumes no valuable time of those punished. Instead of serving time in a brig, where one must be idle, a prisoner puts his shirt back on and returns immediately to duty after the whipping. But Melville objects to this argument on the grounds that all transgressions—many only minor ones—are given equal punishment, which is injustice. For many years, some had suggested taking away the seaman's ration of grog as a substitute for flogging, but Melville points out that sea life is very dreary, and the sailors preferred taking a flogging to losing their grog.

> It is one of the most common punishments for very trivial offenses in the Navy, to stop a seaman's *grog* for a day or a week. And as most seamen so cling to their *grog*, the loss of it is generally deemed by them a very serious penalty. You will sometimes hear them say, "I would rather have my wind *stopped* than my *grog*."[27]

Melville states that there was much more flogging in the United States Navy than in the British Navy. For example,

> the chivalric Virginian, John Randolph of Roanoke, declared, in his place in Congress, that on board the American man-of-war that carried him out [as] Ambassador to Russia he had witnessed more flogging than had taken place on his own plantation of five hundred African slaves in ten years. Certain it is, from what I have personally seen, that the English officers, as a general thing, seem to be less disliked by their crews than the American officers by theirs.[28]

Melville also devotes an entire chapter to "Flogging not Lawful." He argues that, by virtue of an enactment by Congress,

> the Captain is made a legislator, as well as a judge and an executive. So far as it goes, it absolutely leaves to his discretion to decide what things shall be considered crimes, and what shall be the penalty; whether an accused person has been guilty of actions by him declared to be crimes; and how, when, and where

the penalty shall be inflicted. In the American Navy there is an everlasting suspension of the Habeus Corpus.[29]

Melville explains that a captain cannot order more than twelve lashes unless there is a court martial;

> yet, for nearly half a century, this law has been frequently, and with almost perfect impunity, set at naught: though of late, through the exertions of Bancroft [George Bancroft, then Secretary of the Navy, son of Aaron Bancroft, the Unitarian minister in Worcester, Massachusetts] and others, it has been much better observed than formerly; indeed, at the present day, it is generally respected.[30]

Melville's conclusion about the illegality of flogging stated,

> We plant the question, then, on the topmost argument of all, irrespective of incidental considerations, we assert that flogging in the navy is opposed to the essential dignity of man, which no legislator has a right to violate; that it is oppressive, and glaringly unequal in its operations; that it is utterly repugnant to the spirit of our democratic institutions; indeed, that it involves a lingering trait of the worst times of a barbarous feudal aristocracy; in a word, we denounce it as religiously, morally, and immutably *wrong*.[31]

There already was considerable discussion in public forums about flogging in the navy while Melville was writing *White-Jacket*, and a move to cease the practice in the United States Navy as being inhumane had begun. In August, when Melville finished writing the manuscript, the first of five articles on "Flogging in the Navy" by Dr. John A. Lockwood appeared in *The United States Magazine and Democratic Review*. But after *White-Jacket*'s publication, the public's ire was further aroused, and the descriptions that Herman Melville painted served to galvanize the country against the practice. It was stopped very shortly after the book's publication in 1850. It was President James K. Polk, who had appointed George Bancroft to be Secretary of the Navy, who set the stage for the abolition of flogging in the United States Navy.

It is worth noting that Herman Melville also described the chapel on board the *United States*. The accommodations were very poor: there were no chairs; only the gun-rammers and capstan bars placed horizontally upon shot-boxes. Chapel attendance was compulsory regardless of sailors individual religious persuasions. A document called The Articles of War prescribed penalties for not attending divine services. For example, one seaman who claimed to be a Baptist asked to be excused from services because the chaplain was Episcopalian. The sailor was nevertheless required to attend. The boatswains often had to drive the men to chapel services. Melville's character, Jack Chase, captain of the fore top, would joke about the chaplain; "Come boys, don't hang back, . . . come let us go to hear the parson talk about his Lord High Admiral Plato, and Commodore Socrates."[32]

Melville was consumed by wondering—as many have wondered since—how, in a nation that has church and state separated, the state can embrace religion as it does so clearly in its military. In *White-Jacket*, Melville mocks the navy ship chaplain. The present author, having served at sea on an aircraft carrier as a navy chaplain during World War II, was particularly interested in Melville's chapter in "The Chaplain and Chapel in a Man-of-War." The clergyman

> . . . was a slender, middle-aged man, of an amiable deportment and irreproachable conversation; but I must say, that his sermons were ill calculated to benefit the crew. He drank at the mystic fountain of Plato; his head had been turned by the Germans [philosophers]; and this I will say, that White-Jacket himself saw him with Coleridge's *Biographia Literaria* in his hand.[33]

Melville further describes this Emersonian figure.

> Fancy, now, this transcendental divine standing behind a gun-carriage on the main-deck, and addressing five hundred salt-sea sinners upon the psychological phenomena of the soul, and the ontological necessity of every sailor's saving it at all hazards. He enlarged upon the follies of the ancient philosophers; learnedly alluded to the Phaedon of Plato, exposed the follies of Simplicius' Commentary on Aristotle's *De Coelo*, by arraying against that

clever Pagan author of the admired tract of Tertullian—*De Praescriptionibus Haerticorum*—and concluded by a Sanskrit invocation. He was particularly hard upon the Gnostics and Marcionites of the second century of the Christian era.[34]

As he was with the missionaries from America, France, and England that he had met on the South Sea Islands, Melville was disdainful of the navy chaplain, who was similarly ineffectual and too highly educated for his tars. The chaplain's interests were wholly removed from the interests of the sailors on the *Neversink*.

> He never, even in the most remote manner, attacked the every-day vices of the nineteenth century, as eminently illustrated in our man-of-war world. Concerning drunkenness, fighting, flogging, and oppression—things expressly or impliedly prohibited by Christianity—he never said aught.[35]

With the exception of [the chaplain], the purser, was the officer in highest favor with the Commodore, and often conversed together "in a close and confidential manner." Melville comments, "Nor upon reflection, was this to be marveled at, seeing how efficacious, in all despotic governments, it is for the throne and the altar to go hand-in-hand."[36] Melville believed that, if the captain himself was a moral man, "he makes a far better chaplain for his crew than any clergyman can be." This is sometimes illustrated, he wrote, in the case of sloops or armed brigs, which do not have enough of a crew to merit a chaplain. Melville said that such services seemed like family devotions and added, "But our own hearts are our best prayer-rooms, and the chaplains who can most help us are ourselves."[37] Here Melville was expressing the same doctrine that had appeared in Emerson's Divinity School Address of 1838, delivered only a few short years before Melville wrote *White-Jacket*.

Although Herman Melville was disillusioned with the missionaries of the South Seas, finding them inept and destructive of the native culture, and substituting their Christian culture for the native cultures, which Melville did not believe was any better, there are several instances in his life when his concern for social idealism shone forth. He became greatly concerned about human values, the importance of the individual, and what the Industrial Revolution had done and was doing to man's relationship with man. In the concerns of religion many believe that the ethical relationships of person to person are more important than the theological beliefs. In many cases what society does to individuals in a so-called Christian society bears little relationship to the Christian ethics which individuals profess they believe. In this area of society Melville suffered some shocks, of which we have been concerned chiefly about two, the poverty and unconcern for the poor in the city of Liverpool in a country which professed to be a Christian country, and the shocking brutality of the practice of flogging aboard an American man-of-war, again in a country which professed to be primarily Christian in its ethical standards.

C H A P T E R   F O U R

R E A L I T Y
AS SYMBOLIC ALLEGORY

Ralph Waldo Emerson had written that "we fear nothing rightly until we learn the symbolical character of life." Melville took Emerson at his word, and after writing his two South Seas romances, *Typee* and *Omoo*, he turned again to write another such book. But in this case he wrote a book that began as another South Seas story but ended as allegory and symbolism. *Mardi*, in a sense, is a book about a trip in the South Seas, but at the end it is wholly allegorical, the characters are not real, and the book is essentially an attempt to probe some of the deeper aspects of life and of religion.

Tyrus Hillway says of the book, "Though clearly one of the most profound, witty, and charming of this author's novels, [*Mardi*] probably ranks as the least appreciated major American literary work of the nineteenth century."[1] It is a youthful attempt (Herman was in his thirtieth year) to do what later was so nobly done in *Moby-Dick*. Melville was relatively inexperienced at this time in literary craftsmanship.

A reviewer in *The Athenaeum* in London concluded an unfavorable review with these words: " . . . matters become crazier and crazier—more and more foggy—page by page—until the end . . . is felt to be a happy release."[2] Even Richard Henry Dana, Sr. wrote to his son, Richard: "Hasn't Melville written an absurd book? Mr. George Ripley read me a very absurd passage from it yesterday, and speaks of it as a strange compound."[3]

But others found that *Mardi* had a far deeper meaning than some of the reviewers sensed in the novel. F. O. Mattheissen wrote in 1941 that "*Mardi* could serve as source book for reconstructing the conflicting faiths and doubts that were sweeping this country at the end of the eighteen forties."[4]

Tyrus Hillway found much that is constructive in the book. He wrote:

> The book may be regarded as the key to Melville's philosophical, religious, political, and social ideas during the most significant and productive period of his career. In it are found in rich detail—albeit in allegorical form—the penetrating speculations and comments of a brilliant and energetic young mind upon some of the monumental problems of human history.[5]

Raymond Weaver wrote that "the riddle of *Mardi* goes near to the heart of the riddle of Melville's life."[6] But he added that "there is infinite laughter in the book—but the laughter is at bottom the laughter of despair."[7] Although Melville was now a husband and a father, there were deeper things which were churning in his inner life which did not always appear on the surface.

Actually these years around the middle of the century were some of the best and happiest years of Herman Melville's life. His first two books *Typee* and *Omoo* had been successes. He had decided at this moment in his life that perhaps after all he could earn a living and support a growing family with his literary efforts. He had married and had set up housekeeping with his bride, Elizabeth, and several relatives in New York City, the city of his birth. He certainly believed that his third book would bring him universal recognition.

But he was to be shocked and disappointed. For *Mardi* was not welcomed with the plaudits that his first two books had been. One reviewer called it "rubbishing rhapsody," and this critic was not alone. There was almost universal rejection. Many believed that his adventures into allegory had been the wrong tack. The first two books had been authored as if they were factual accounts of Melville's actual life in the South Seas. But from about chapter sixty-five onward, *Mardi* ceases to be a plausible tale of adventure and becomes an allegorical commentary on a series of deep philosophical speculations. It is centered around the search for the beautiful maiden Yillah, who like Fayaway and many of Melville's female characters, is lightly documented as to character. She personifies divine truth, and the story is typical of the hero's travels through the world from country to country in which are revealed all sorts of people, beliefs, and customs.

Merrill R. Davis divides the book into three distinct parts which he terms "Narrative Beginning," "The Romantic Interlude," and the "Travelogue-Satire."[8] The first thirty-eight chapters are the "Narrative Beginning," and many have felt that if Melville had only extended this part of the book and ended it there, he might have had a good travel book like his first two successful novels. The "Romantic Interlude," takes up the next twenty-six chapters. A new set of characters is introduced, and a romantic love story is told. The third section, the "Travelogue-Satire," is the part of the book that completely turned almost everyone against it. With almost no warning, the reader is subjected to satirical allegory. Here a third group of characters appears, and from here on to the conclusion of the book, the reader embarks upon a chartless voyage. Yet, it is this last section which is of the most interest to us when we consider Melville's changing religious ideas.

Edwin Haviland Miller calls these three sections simply "a narrative, a romance, and a satirical travelogue with meta-physico-socio overtones."[9]

There have been many hypotheses as to why Melville changed course in the middle of *Mardi*, abandoned his successful style of writing seafaring tales, and embarked upon an allegorical tale. "Allegory is a figurative representation conveying a meaning other than and in addition to the literal."[10] An allegory is more sustained than a metaphor, and a fable or a parable is a short allegory with one definite moral, as the parables of Jesus, although sometimes it is difficult for modern interpreters to understand the definite meaning of some of Jesus' parables. It has been a favorite form of expression in much of world literature. Bunyan's *Pilgrim's Progress* is perhaps the best known allegorical piece of literature. Now Herman Melville embarked upon this kind of expression, and in *Mardi* he made feeble attempts at what became such mature allegorizing in *Moby-Dick*.

We have already stated that for the purposes of looking at Herman Melville's religious ideas the last third, the allegorical part of *Mardi*, is of the greatest interest. It is well worth looking at some of this allegorical tale, in particular about the island of Serenia.

The cast of characters is interesting. Taji starts out as the narrator of the tale and the hero, but he takes a smaller and smaller part in the dialogue which emerges, and at the end he is almost non-existent as a person of importance. The pages are interspersed with verses of the poet laureate, Yoomy.

Lewis Mumford says,

> When Taji sits down with the five-and-twenty kings, the invocation to wine is about at the level of Peacock's drinking songs: and the poorest of Yoomy's songs are poetry only by typographic courtesy. These are all faults; and not little ones; but what means infinitely more is the fact that a brave, vigorous spirit presides over *Mardi*, appraising all the evil and injustice and superstition and ugliness in the world, as they masquerade under the guise of religion and patriotism, and economic prudence and political necessity. In *Mardi*, one begins to feel Melville's range, and his depth.[11]

Melville also discovered when he wrote *Mardi* the nature of the demon in his own soul, the deeper half which the character Babbalanja called Azzageddi. Babbalanja reflected the ideas of Melville's own time and America, the contemporary propaganda to be explicit. Babbalanja was a thoughtful Christian, a typical republican, "who met adversity with a jest or a wry smile, who drank brandy with Mr. Duyckinck, and who paid his respects with genteel punctuality to all the Gansevoorts and Melvilles and Shaws."[12]

But Melville also discovered within his own self a deeper self; that he was not a man of his time, but a person who saw the follies of his own age.

> This deeper Melville did not altogether supplant the man of convention; they do not represent several and successive phases

of growth: but, as Melville suggests in *Moby-Dick*, they represented aspects of a cycle through which one goes again and again, never reaching a terminus, no ultimate point of rest, or resolution.[13]

This aspect of Melville's thought is represented in *Mardi* as the character Azzageddi, who asks all of the questions that Melville the philosopher wants to ask. It is he who speaks from within the man. In every aspect of his conventional life Azzageddi speaks to Melville. For example, Melville continues to socialize with his friend Duyckinck, but at the same time this inner spirit asks some questions about the ultimate as contrasted with the socially correct.

Yet, the character Azzageddi was free only in the worst sense of freedom, because he was irresponsible. Nothing will prevent him from making these criticisms of the conventional. He constantly intrudes upon every thought to ask whether it is important, or whether is represents the Eternal, or as Plato would say, the Ideal. In *Mardi* the misuse of this freedom is not so apparent. In *Moby-Dick*, the hauling up out of the depths many of these impossible questions made real the creation of a literary masterpiece, while in *Pierre* this same freedom worked out to reveal the bottomless pit of Melville's unconscious mind, and it led to a disastrous concept of human relationships.

But Azzageddi's nature is the impulse felt by many persons to be critical of what they see around them, all of the two-faced things that are being done in the name of religion, patriotism, social welfare, and in almost every area of human concern. This is the spirit that worked so well in *Moby-Dick* to work out the destiny of Ahab and his monomania. In *Clarel*, it takes the form of endless questions that have no answers.

Melville found this deeper spirit in the allegorical parts of *Mardi*, and it became his passion, so that when Nathaniel Hawthorne and he talked together, Hawthorne felt that Herman was always asking the impossible questions. This trait of seeking his deeper self was probably always present in Herman Melville's consciousness from his teenage years, but it never surfaced in his literary works, except in the criticism of the missionaries in *Typee* and *Omoo*. In writing *Mardi*, Melville began to find his deeper nature. Its literary expression did not please the critics nor the public who preferred the conventional, and his abject rejection by the public in the poor reception of his third novel drove him back to writing the potboilers that the public loved—for purely economic reasons.

One of the most interesting parts of *Mardi* comes towards the end of the book, probably when most have already given up the plot and the novel as a hopeless morass. It is the landing of the third group of characters on the island of Serenia which give us some insights into Melville's personal religious ideas. The travelers were greeted as they landed. "Emerging from beneath the trees there came a goodly multitude in flowing robes; palm-branches in their hands; and as they came they sang,

> Hail voyagers, hail!
> Whence e'er ye come, where'er ye rove,
> No calmer strand,
> No sweeter land
> Will e'er ye view than the Land of Love!"[14]

Thus begins the account of the visit to the island of Serenia. It is well to note that Melville was not beyond portraying things Biblical in the same way that a modern Cecil B. de Mille might in one of his religious movie extravaganzas. Note that the language is in Biblical King James English, and people are in flowing robes and carry palm branches. The people on this island of Serenia believe in Oro, the Father of all, (read God) and in Alma, the master, which is simply another name for the Christ figure.

F. O. Mattheissen wrote:

It would be even more difficult to say precisely what Melville believed on the basis of his treatment of religion in *Mardi*. So far as this book has a resolution, it lies in Babbalanja's finding peace at last in the Christian state of Serenia. Although the church is corrupt in the rest of *Mardi*, here "right reason" and Alma

(Christ) are held to be the same. Here though the people do not believe in man's perfection, they do not regard him as "absolutely set" against all good. Here, too, the social state, though also imperfect, at least is not based on making "the miserable many support the happy few."[15]

There is only love on this island, no oppression. There is some skepticism on the part of the travelers about all of this, but they are told that Alma must not be judged "by all those who profess his faith."[16] One traveler expresses the idea that "so long even from my infancy have I witnessed the wrongs committed in his name, that thinking all evil must flow from a congenial fountain, I have scorned to study the whole record of your master's life. By parts I only know it."

When asked if the people of Serenia live up to the ideals that their master spoke, the reply is "nothing do we claim, we but earnestly endeavor." When asked how they treat those who dissent from belief in Alma, the reply is that "if he dissent from us, we then equally dissent from him: and man's faculties are Oro-given. Nor will we say that he is wrong and we are right, for this we know not absolutely." Here Melville, of course, is making a contrast with and some satire upon the missionaries who are converting the heathen because they know that they are right and the heathen are wrong. The Serenians "look for creeds in actions, which are the truthful symbols of the things within . . . He who prays every hour to Alma but does live with love is more an unbeliever than the person who rejects the master but does his living according to the master's precepts."

When confronted again with the missionary theology that Alma teaches something wholly new, "a revelation of things before unimagined," the Serenians reply that all that is vital in the master's faith was lived long before the master's coming. The ideas of truth, justice and love are not the revelations of Alma alone. They were known. The difference is that Alma opens up their hearts.

The discussion then turns towards the method of rule in the Serenia. They have no king because Alma rebukes the arrogance of place and power. They do not believe in man's perfection. In Alma's heart there is a germ "that we seek to foster. To that we cling; else all were hopeless." On their island "the miserable many do not support the happy few." Nor do they seek to breed equality by breeding anarchy. "Equality is not for all." Such differences must be. The needy are supplied by the bounty. "But none starve outright while others feast." They make the vicious dwell apart until reclaimed. Their laws are not of the vengeance kind, but love and Alma.

The visitors then ask if Alma is divine because they found no temples on the island. The response to this is that "this isle is all one temple of his praise; every leaf is consecrated his." This sounds a little Emersonian, God in all things.

Ask if the islanders fast and pray, and the answer is, "We never fast and pray and stand and sing, as at long intervals." This, of course, is a comment on the long services conducted by the Protestant missionaries. And then a comment about the Catholic services: others supplicate their gods with censors. They also have no priests, but one, and he is Alma himself. "We have his precepts, we seek no comments but our hearts." Their faith has lived on without priests and temples. "What we believe, we hold divine, and things divine endure forever."

The Serenians also believe that "right reason and Alma are the same; else Alma, not reason, we would reject . . . The master's great command is love; and here do all things wise and all things good unite. Love is all in all. The more we love the more we know; and so reversed."

"When Alma dwelt in Mardi, it was with the poor and friendless. He fed the famishing; he healed the sick; he bound up wounds. For every precept that he spoke, he did ten thousand mercies. And Alma is our loved example." Alma not only spoke for the poor and the friendless, but he also challenged the authorities, the great chieftains, and he told them all their pride was vanity, and bade them ask their souls. "In me cried, 'is that heart of mild content which in vain ye seek in rank and title? I am love; love ye then me.'"

Melville concludes this section of *Mardi*:

With swimming eyes the old man kneeled, and round him grouped king, sage, gray hairs and youth. There as they kneeled, and as the old man blessed them, the setting sun burst forth from mists, gilded the island round about, shed rays upon their heads, and went down in a glory—all the east radiant with red burnings like an altar fire.[17]

Why the travelers ever wanted to depart from Serenia is a deep mystery. They had been looking for an ideal spot on the face of the Pacific Ocean, and seemingly they had found it. Perhaps the piety had gotten a bit sticky, and they were burdened down by it. But it is worthwhile to note the kind of religion which seemed to appeal to Melville, for I do not see how one can read this section except as Melville's approving the kind of religion which is expressed therein. It has all of the aspects of his future mature Unitarian view. Alma is not divine. Only Oro is divine. It has something of Emersonian paganism in it with everything becoming divine as it partakes of Alma. It does not make a fetish of the Scriptures. These ideas existed long before Alma came. The test of religion is not what creed one recites, but how one treats one's fellow men, the essence of Unitarian and of Jesus' belief. And one does not believe that he has the final truth, and certainly he will not persecute those who disagree with his own precepts. All of this is looked upon favorably by Melville in these passages in *Mardi*. It illustrates a kind of ideal religion which Melville could accept, and it is far removed from the kind that he found among the missionaries of the South Seas or in the Dutch Reformed Church.

Melville is much concerned to illustrate in *Mardi* the point of view that human beings are incapable of grasping the absolute.

Each of the three protagonists in this trilogy and the answers offered by religion and philosophy inadequate and unsatisfactory. Each develops a great contempt for a world in which a tragic disparity exists between man's avowed beliefs and his actual conduct. Each becomes convinced of the utter falsity of—ready-made creeds but is nevertheless restless in his unbelief.[18]

In this third part of the novel one can readily understand that Herman Melville is still wrestling with his childhood Calvinistic teachings, and is rejecting not only Calvinism but any fixed system of beliefs which is not open-ended to new truth. Actually, three of Melville's novels, *Mardi*, *Moby-Dick*, and *Pierre* express the futility of the human search for truth. On the other hand, *Clarel*, and *Billy Budd*, although they present an evil world and the reality of evil, still contain the belief that there are ideals worth striving for.

"[Melville] simply acknowledged the fact that, in the present world, man's innate weakness prevents him from reaching the heights which in the future he may aspire to and win."[19] But notice that it is not original sin which prevents man from reaching his aspirations. It is simply man's limitedness, his inability in his present stage of existence to think clearly through philosophical problems and to come up with a definite answer that does not conspire against the intellect. So by the time that he wrote *Mardi*, Melville had moved a long way from Calvinism.

One cannot understand Melville's thought about religion without knowing something of the religious situation in America in the middle years of the nineteenth century. The fundamentalist beliefs of Calvinism and of all religious systems were being challenged by the new discoveries of science. Geology said that the world was not created in seven days; bones were being dug up all over the world which showed ancient creatures of the past, now extinct, even several extinct species of man or man-like creatures. Astronomy was beginning to move toward the quantum leap that it would take in another fifty years, and then another leap fifty years later. It was difficult to believe in the Garden of Eden story literally. Biblical scholars in Europe, particularly in Germany, were beginning to question many of the names that were assigned as authors to many of the books of the Bible. It was a time of religious scientific ferment.

Tyrus Hillway writes,

> Consequently, [Melville] abandoned his religious faith as it had
> been taught him during childhood. He continued, however, a
> careful and devoted study of Christianity throughout his life,
> perhaps hoping to recover the faith which he had lost.[20]

Later in 1857, Melville was to undertake a trip to the Holy
Land to see that country for himself, and to walk in the paths
of the religious greats of the Moslem, Jewish, and Christian
religions. We shall document this later when we consider the
great poem that resulted from the trip—*Clarel*.

Tyrus Hillway concludes his study with these words:

> *Mardi* ends in the failure to discover truth but not in the relin-
> quishment of the quest. Taji, the hero, still retains belief in the
> invincibility of the human intellect. He has observed that most
> established religions are insincere if not fraudulent . . . He has
> visited only one place on earth which promises a life of decency
> and contentment—the island of Serenia, where men live quietly
> and peacefully according to the original teachings of Christ,
> without pomp and pretense, without arguments over creeds and
> theories, and in a tolerant brotherliness. But on Serenia there is
> no Yillah, no revelation of divine truth. Men live resigned to the
> fact that they must remain ignorant of the true reasons for their
> existence.[21]

This endeavor to get back to the original teachings of Jesus
of Nazareth, so evident in Melville's ideas in *Mardi*, was a
strong strain in Unitarianism during Melville's lifetime. Even
Thomas Jefferson, whom some term a Unitarian because he
said that he believed that before he died every young man in
America would become a Unitarian, undertook with scissors
and paste to reconstruct the New Testament Gospels.
Jefferson eventually published what today we call the *Jefferson
Bible*. He called it *The Life and Morals of Jesus of Nazareth*.
Jefferson eliminated everything but the actual sayings of Jesus
as they are recorded in Matthew, Mark, Luke, and John. He
eliminated anything which appeared to him to be an accre-
tion.

Although certainly not well-received by religious people in Jefferson's time, even today scholars believe that the transmission of the Gospel text is far more complicated than Jefferson conceived it to be. There was not an original pure Gospel, and one cannot just eliminate what one terms accretions and get back to the authentic words of Jesus himself. There are more fundamental questions about the text itself which more nearly represents what people thought about Jesus from A.D. 65 to the end of the first century rather than what Jesus actually preached.

Although many modern Unitarians are not particularly interested in Jesus, in the nineteenth century there was a strong movement among many Unitarians to get back to original Christianity, to recover Christianity as it was before it had a theological and mysterious overlay, and a definite creedal theology. This must have appealed to Herman Melville, for he depicted the residents of Serenia as living by this simple Gospel.

Eighteen forty-nine was also an important year in Melville's life, for his son Malcolm was born on 16 February. *Mardi* was published in March by Richard Bentley in London. In September, Bentley published *Redburn*, the account of Melville's voyage ten years previously to Liverpool. In October, Melville sailed to London to arrange for the publication of *White-Jacket*, the book that came out of his eighteen-month stint in the United States Navy.

Melville had to admit that his first excursion into allegory had been a dismal economic failure. Yet it was an experiment in writing that was to have profound results on his future masterpiece: The writing of *Mardi* eventuated in one of the greatest allegorical tales of all times, *Moby-Dick*. But whatever happened, it changed Melville's whole outlook on writing, and his rapport with his audience. Perhaps he believed that through allegory and satire he could tell truths that were deeper than travel accounts. Both Melville and his friend Evert Duyckinck expected *Mardi* to be a great American classic. In this expectation they were extremely disappointed.

Mardi sold only thirty-nine hundred copies during Melville's lifetime.

Perhaps Edwin Haviland Miller best expressed the paradox of *Mardi* when he wrote,

> There will probably never be a satisfactory interpretation of *Mardi*. It will always remain a work in which the seams are showing, the symbols interpreted according to the disposition of the interpreter. There are delightful interludes, amusing discussions, some interesting satire. Yet it is a wild, undisciplined work as headstrong and romantic as Taji himself. Melville muffles the psychological drama through comic tactics and through seemingly intellectual discussions, although the papier-mâché characters enthuse rather than think, indulge in sophomoric witticisms rather than in serious, logical discussion. Melville writes from no preconceived position; he is groping for answers as he writes.[22]

F. O. Mattheissen offers an excuse for *Mardi*:

> It is hardly surprising that Melville's efforts in his book are frequently turgid and confused. Here he was not in control; he possessed no disciplined knowledge of philosophy, and was often whirled about by his abstractions.[23]

We now will turn to the writing of Melville's masterpiece and one of the greatest novels in American literature, *Moby-Dick*.

C H A P T E R   F I V E

HUMANISM & ALLEGORY:
M O B Y - D I C K

In 1850, seeking some relief from the summer heat of New York City and perhaps from the crowded Melville household, Herman Melville, Elizabeth, and their young son Malcolm fled the city and went to Pittsfield. They boarded with Thomas Melvill's widow where Herman had spent a year as a boy working on the farm. He visited the Shaker Village at Hancock, Massachusetts, a few miles away, and most importantly, he got a copy of Nathaniel Hawthorne's *Mosses from an Old Manse*. He had not yet met Hawthorne, although Melville had admired his work and mentioned him in *White-Jacket*. On 5 August 1850, the two men met for the first time on an all-day excursion with Evert Duyckinck and Oliver Wendell Holmes, who both summered near Pittsfield. Melville and Hawthorne took an immediate liking to each other, and as a result, Melville hurriedly read *Mosses*, and wrote an enthusiastic review of the book. Evert Duyckinck took a copy of the review back with him to New York City for publication in his magazine, *Literary World*.

In this review we begin to get something of the maturity of the point of view of *Moby-Dick*, on which Melville was now working. Melville believed that an author must have suffered himself in order to depict it in others. He found a power of blackness in Hawthorne's writing. He believed that Hawthorne probed not only with his intellect but also with his heart. Melville had been reading Shakespeare during these years, and he found in Hawthorne's writings something of the same vital truth of the power of evil that Shakespeare depicted in many of his characters. Melville was able to speak in

Moby-Dick through the character of Ishmael and Ahab about his own preoccupation with the reality of evil.

To some of the readers of the *Literary World*, to compare Hawthorne with Shakespeare must have seemed a bit of extravagant praise. But Melville was simply presaging his own deeper feelings which were to emerge so beautifully in *Moby-Dick*.

Melville so enjoyed the area around Pittsfield that in September the family decided not to return to New York City, and Herman bought an adjoining farm which he called "Arrowhead" because of some Indian artifacts or arrowheads which he discovered there. "Broadhall," his aunt's home where he stayed before the purchase of "Arrowhead," had already been sold, or he might have purchased that farm which he loved so much. By October of 1850, the three Melvilles were joined by his mother and four sisters who left New York City and moved to "Arrowhead." He tried to do some farming, but he discovered that he was not really cut out to be a farmer, although he did bring in the crops in October. Then he eagerly resumed his writing.

He was also encouraged to start a new novel by the good reviews which *White-Jacket* had received and which came to his attention at this time. There was some criticism of the way in which Melville had described the religious activities on board the *Neversink*. But Melville in *White-Jacket* had not pretended that he was giving a totally accurate picture of his own experiences. He was more interested in showing the navy's disregard for the welfare of the common seaman. So he had used satire and caricature in the novel, and this was especially true of the picture which he gave of the chaplain of the ship.

White-Jacket received a very favorable review in *The Athenaeum*. Henry F. Chorley wrote,

> We cannot recall another novelist or sketcher who has given the poetry of the ship—her voyages and her crew—in a manner at all resembling his . . . Mr. Melville's sea-creatures, calms and storms, belong to the more dreamy tone of *The Ancient Mariner*, and have a touch of serious and suggestive picturesqueness appertaining to a world of art higher than the actor's or the scene-painter's.[1]

In *John Bull* the reviewer wrote,

> The pleasing fact remains that the rattling youngster has grown into a thoughtful man, who without any abatement of his rich and ever sparkling wit, has obtained the mastery of his own fancy.[2]

George Ripley reviewed the book for the *New York Daily Tribune* and wrote in part:

> Mr. Melville has performed an excellent service in revealing the secrets of his prison-house, and calling the public attention to the indescribable abominations of the naval life, reeking with the rankest corruption, cruelty, and blood . . . A man of Melville's brain and pen is a dangerous character in the presence of a gigantic humbug.[3]

In order to write this new novel, Melville established a routine for himself. He awakened at eight, fed his horse and cow, had his breakfast, and then lit a fire in the fireplace in his study. He wrote until mid-afternoon, at which time Elizabeth summoned him to dinner. Because of his weak eyes, he could not write in the evening as it was too much of a strain. During the winter of 1850-1851, Melville read a great deal of what Hawthorne had written. By the end of May, he felt that the book was fairly well done. It is interesting to note that his old ship the *Acushnet* was wrecked that summer in the North Atlantic off Saint Lawrence Island on her third voyage. Reading of this tragedy must have encouraged him in his writing.

The rights for publication for the book were negotiated by his brother Allan, who acted as his agent. He negotiated a contract with Harper and Brothers. Herman shipped off the pages also to Bentley in London for a British edition. Melville had decided to call the novel *Moby-Dick*, but in England it was published as *The Whale*. Melville dedicated the book to Hawthorne who had encouraged him to dig deeply into his own inner soul in writing the book.

So much has been written about *Moby-Dick*, that it does not seem worthwhile for our purposes to say much about its contents as we look at the religious ideas of Herman Melville. The book, of course, is very much about religion as Captain Ahab and the crew, including Ishmael, (read Melville) search for the white whale that had in a previous voyage taken off one of Captain Ahab's lower legs. The story centers around the monomaniac passion of Ahab to find the white whale and to harpoon him, thus setting up the tragedy of the loss of the ship and all aboard except Ishmael.

But there are some elements of *Moby-Dick* with which we cannot help but be concerned if we want to understand Melville's religious ideas. One of the great chapters of the book is the sermon by Reverend Mudge at the Seaman's Bethel in New Bedford. We shall be concerned about that for it is supposed by many to be a very Calvinistic sermon. It would seem to the author that at best the sermon could be called neo-Calvinistic, that is, a modified Calvinism. One of the strongest tenets of original Calvinism were the ideas of election and predestination, that is that individuals were elected by God to be saved or to be damned, and that this was predestined, and that one could do nothing about it. There is none of this in Father Mapple's sermon. The Calvinists, as the years went by, in many instances gave up the ideas of election and predestination, and spoke enthusiastically about the greatness of God and the littleness of man. There is a great deal of this in the sermon of Father Mapple. But many theologians other than John Calvin have had this kind of a theological perspective about God's greatness and man's littleness. I believe that it is a mistake to automatically label this idea as Calvinistic, for it is not necessarily Calvinistic teaching if one's God has these virtues (or lack of them).

One of the finest sermons ever written was composed not by John Eliot or Jonathan Edwards or any other Calvinist preacher, but by Herman Melville when writing *Moby-Dick*. This is the rather extensive sermon in chapter nine of *Moby-Dick*, delivered by Father Mapple before Ishmael (Melville) went to sea in the *Acushnet*. The question which must be raised about this sermon of Father Mapple is whether it represented the religious views with which Melville was indoctrinated when he was a child and teenager, or whether Melville wrote the sermon long after he himself had given up such ideas. Many believe that it is a masterpiece of literary work but did not represent the views of Melville himself at the time that it was written.

Scholars differ in their interpretation of this matter. I personally, although I am not a professional Melville scholar, would believe that this is a fine literary exercise by a great writer trying to show the kind of sermons which were delivered to seamen in the New Bedford whaling chapel at the time that the fictitious *Pequod* put to sea. I would argue that by the time *Moby-Dick* was being written by Herman Melville in the early 1850s, his own religious ideas had changed drastically, and that by this period in his life Melville was very skeptical about religion in general. He had been disillusioned by the missionaries in his South Seas travels, and for years he had been questioning the theology of John Calvin.

Many persons brought up with as conservative a theological background as was Melville go through an odyssey to more liberal ideas fairly easily, but Herman Melville struggled with these ideas throughout his life, including the period during the writing of *Clarel* which was published in 1876, fifteen years before his death. Some persons, of course, live happily with such theological ideas. But Melville was an overly-thoughtful man in his concerns about good and evil and the providence of God.

In *Moby-Dick and Calvinism*, T. Walter Herbert Jr. expresses the conviction that at the time of writing the novel, Melville himself was in the midst of a disintegration of the theological view of Calvinism which had dominated early nineteenth-century America. Professor Herbert noted that Melville read both orthodox Calvinists and more liberal views such as those expounded by the Unitarians, and that he was torn and grasped by the controversy in his own soul. He believes that Calvinism pervades the novel, but that it is twisted and turned upside down as Melville dismantles its authority. Melville's own turmoil finds expression in several of the characters of *Moby-Dick*, each of whom exhibits an inner religious turmoil; Captain Ahab, Ishmael, and some of the other characters in the novel.

Instead of setting a confident new spiritual course, Melville leaves us with the great shroud of the sea rolling on as in immemorial ages. It is the image of an eternal mystery, thus assuring that the human spirit will never exhaust its materials, never lose its opportunity to deal directly with the unfathomable terror and abundance of life.[4]

Some have believed, I think mistakenly, that Herman Melville incorporated his own religious beliefs into the sermon. Actually, the sermon is a magnificent summary of some of the teachings of Calvinism which laid the basis for Ahab's futile chase of the great white whale, Moby-Dick. Yet the language is not theological but very much in the seaman's milieu.

Melville wrote that Father Mapple "was in the hardy winter of a healthy old age."[5] "He quietly approached the pulpit." Melville says that the chapel architect, upon the suggestion of Father Mapple, had "finished the pulpit without a stairs, substituting a perpendicular ladder like those used in mounting a ship from a boat at sea." Father Mapple "mounted the steps as if ascending the main-top of his vessel." He began by uttering a "prayer so devout that he seemed kneeling and praying at the bottom of the sea."

The sermon was based upon the Old Testament book of Jonah, and Father Mapple took as his text the last verse of the first chapter of Jonah, "and God prepared a great fish to swallow up Jonah." Mapple suggested that what the book of Jonah taught was "a two-stranded" lesson, "a lesson to us all as sinful men, and a lesson to me (Father Mapple) as a pilot of the living God." Jonah "with this sin of disobedience in him" seeks to flee from God. He thinks that this ship will take him to countries where "God does not reign." The captain of the ship tests Jonah's determination by charging him three times the normal fare to Tarshish. Jonah goes into the bowels of the ship to sleep. A furious storm arises, and the sailors are suspicious that it is Jonah who has brought them this bad luck.

The sailors drew lots; Jonah lost, and was thrown over-board into a raging sea. There he was swallowed by a big fish. The Bible does not say the fish was a whale. "Observe his prayer" in the "belly of the fish," and learn a weighty lesson. "For sinful as he is Jonah does not weep and wail for direct deliverance. He feels that his dreadful punishment is just. He leaves all his deliverance to God . . . grateful for punishment." Jonah, said Father Mapple, was "a model for repentance." That is a central tenet of Calvinism, but also the conviction of many other branches of the Christian religion.

Then Father Mapple drove home his point: "Shipmates, God has laid but one hand upon you; both his hands press upon me." But Jonah was thrown up by the fish on to the dry land. "Tarshish he never reached." But the lesson was clear.

Woe to that pilot of the living God who slights it. Woe to him whom this world charms from Gospel duty! Woe to him who seeks to pour oil upon the waters when God has brewed them into a gale! Woe to him who seeks to please rather than to appall! Woe to him whose good name is more to him than goodness. Woe to him who, in this world, courts not dishonor. Woe to him who would not be true, even though to be false were salvation. Yes, woe to him who, as the great Pilot Paul has it, while preaching to others is himself a castaway.

Father Mapple brings his sermon to a conclusion with another great burst of oratory:

Is not the main-truck higher than the kelson is low? Delight in him—a far, far upward and inward delight—who against the proud gods and commodores of this earth, ever stands forth his own inexorable self. Delight is to him whose strong arms yet support him, when the ship of this base treacherous world has gone down beneath him. Delight in him who gives no quarter to the truth, and kills, burns, and destroys all sin though he pluck it from under the robes of Senators and Judges. Delight—top-gallant delight is to him, who acknowledges no law or lord, but the Lord his God, and he is only a patriot to heaven. Delight is to him, whom all the waves of the billows of the seas of the boister-ous mob can never shake from this sure Keel of the Ages. And eternal delight and deliciousness will be his, who coming to lay him down, can say with his final breath, O Father, chiefly known to me by Thy rod, mortal or immortal, here I die. Yet this is nothing; I leave eternity to Thee; for what is man that he should live out the lifetime of his God.

What a magnificent sermon this is, and so appropriate for seamen leaving on a whaler the next day for a long voyage to parts unknown and for an indefinite time span. This is not a sermon with Calvinistic theology expounded as such. The seamen would scarcely listen to a theological sermon. Father Taylor of Boston was once asked why he had formed the Seaman's Mission in Boston with a great deal of Unitarian financial help, and he replied that seamen would not go to hear the lofty William Ellery Channing at the Federal Street Church.

All of the undertones and overtones of Father Mapple's sermon speak of the religion of Melville's childhood, the Calvinistic Dutch Reformed faith which he was to abandon or had already abandoned when he began to think for himself. Especially manifest in the sermon is the sovereignty of God. Everything is subject to the will of God. Melville has moved beyond the Calvinistic idea that it is a whim of God who will be saved and who will gain glory in Heaven. The real message of the sermon is that Jonah discovered that God is everywhere. He could not escape God by going to Tarshish. God is a universal being and not just the God of the Jews in Palestine.

Whether the preacher, Reverend Enoch Mudge at the Whaleman's Chapel, whom Melville describes as Father Mapple in New Bedford was the inspiration for this sermon or whether perhaps Melville heard the preaching of Father Taylor at the Seaman's Mission in Boston after his return from the voyage to the South Seas, is not known. But it is a question that we will now address.

There are at least two good possibilities as to the prototype of Father Mapple in *Moby-Dick*. There can be little question that Melville probably attended a service in the chapel before he went a'whaling. His own ship the *Acushnet* was fitting out in Fairhaven just across New Bedford Harbor.

Professor Curtis Dahl, speaking on the occasion of the two hundredth anniversary of the birth of the Reverend Enoch Mudge, the first chaplain of the Seaman's Bethel in New Bedford, on 20 June 1976, asked,

> But what of vigorous sounding, old Methodist sounding Father Mapple? Was he a character wholly created by Melville, or was there a real Father Mapple? Certainly there was no one at the New Bedford Bethel by that name. Certainly much about him was quarried out of Melville's rich imagination. With his sailor-like yet Old Testament prophet air, with his vigor and sincerity and salty speech, he is surely one of the great created characters of American fiction.[6]

It is worthwhile to examine the possibilities of a role model. The first possibility is Enoch Mudge. But "Enoch Mudge was no Mapple, and no Taylor. He did not have their rhetoric and fire; he did not play to the audience. He was not a dramatic preacher."[7] He had never been to sea, though he wrote and preached to the seamen. Though he was not an orator, Curtis Dahl believes of Mudge

> in his quiet competent way he may have done far more for his hundreds of mariner "sons" than any Mapple or even Taylor could. His able conscientious hard work, his executive ability, his talent for writing, his genius for getting on with all kinds of people . . . laid the foundations of the successful ministry that the Port Society still continues after so many years.[8]

> He was the first chaplain of the Society, and he had dedication and courage. He was called a Methodist of the Methodists. When he came to New Bedford in 1832, he had had a great deal of ministerial experience. He was accepted into the Methodist ministry at the age of seventeen or eighteen in 1793. It may, moreover have been with his Methodist contacts with—who else but Father Taylor himself—that led to his appointment in New Bedford. He replaced Father Taylor in the Methodist church in Ipswich, Massachusetts. Dahl says that the proof is not conclusive about this matter, "But the evidence points that way."[9]

Another possibility for a prototype for Father Mapple is Father Taylor. He was a famous preacher, chaplain of the

Seaman's Bethel in Boston. He had a wide reputation, and in many ways was something of a tourist attraction, like Fanuel Hall, Old North Church, or King's Chapel. Charles Dickens, Harriet Martineau, Walt Whitman, and many other famous people went to hear him. A Unitarian preacher, Ralph Waldo Emerson, said that "he was the work of the same hand that made Demosthenes, Shakespeare, and Burns."[10] It is certainly probable that by 1851 when Melville wrote *Moby-Dick* he had heard Father Taylor on one of his many visits to Boston. In fact Lizzie's father, Judge Lemuel Shaw, was probably one of the many prominent Unitarians of Boston who helped finance the Seamen's Bethel, for the Unitarians realized that they could not draw the seamen to their sophisticated churches.

In his youth Taylor had been a seaman before he entered the Methodist ministry. Like Father Mapple, he used references to the sea and sailors and ships when he preached. He had great wit and sincerity.

> He was a robust, colorful, outgoing character with not a little of the play actor in him. In the pulpit he had great skill. He could build up excitement to an intense pitch and then break it at just the right time with a telling epigrammatic remark. He was, Edward Everett once said, "a walking Bethel."[11]

In fact, Father Taylor, in spite of all of his non-Unitarian theology was very popular among Unitarian ministers and laymen in Boston, and often he was invited to the annual May Meetings of the American Unitarian Association to lead in prayer. The Unitarians waxed with literary zeal in their prayers, but Father Taylor moved them more emotionally than their own ministers.

> The Boston Chapel did not have a ship pulpit, but neither did the New Bedford chapel. That is a fiction from Melville's mind. But the Boston Bethel "did have hanging behind the minister a vivid painting of a ship in a storm. If one must find a source for the fictional Mapple . . . Taylor must be the choice. And a great source he was."[12]

It is not the purpose nor the province of this book to deal at length with the contents of *Moby-Dick* except as they apply to the religious and philosophical ideas of Herman Melville. The book is so well-known and so much has been written about it in this century that it is difficult for most of us to realize that it had a poor reception when it was published in 1851, and throughout most of the nineteenth century. A few critics hinted at its greatness. It was not appreciated because it was so much at odds with the current thinking of the day. In liberal religious circles the doctrine of organic evolution which was expounded just a few years after the publication of *Moby-Dick* by Charles Darwin's great book *The Origin of Species*, produced a kind of optimism that was very foreign to Melville's thinking.

It has been said, and I believe truly, that Melville was strangely prescient of the points of view of the twentieth century rather than his own. In the same vein, George Bernard Shaw's idea which saw man moving upward and onward until he attained the stature of a superman belongs in the latter half of the nineteenth century rather than in the twentieth century. Shaw lived until 1950, so he spent a lot of his lifetime in this century. But Herman Melville who lived in the nineteenth century had many ideas which became prominent in our century.

Beginning with the American Renaissance, as F. O. Matthiessen terms it, in the time of Ralph Waldo Emerson, the doctrine was expounded that evil was simply the lack of good, and that evil had no meaning except as an opposite of the good. It reached its greatest climax in the religious world in the works of Mary Baker Eddy and Christian Science. This point of view was not professed by Herman Melville. He believed that evil was real, very real, and that it caused tragedy in the world.

Matthiessen says in his landmark work:

> The creation of tragedy demands of its author a mature understanding of the relation of the individual to society, and, more especially, of the nature of good and evil. He must have a coher-

ent grasp of social forces, or, at least, of man as a social being; otherwise he will possess no frame of reference within which to make actual his dramatic conflicts. For the hero of tragedy is never merely an individual, he is a man of action, in conflict with other individuals in a definite social order.[13]

Matthiessen also believes that "tragedy does not pose the situation of a faultless individual (or class) overwhelmed by an evil world, for it is built on the experienced realization that man is radically imperfect."[14] Yet this same man must be capable, for there to be genuine tragedy, to be able to apprehend perfection. He believed that "he must be as far from the chaos of despair as he is free from ill founded optimism."[15]

Ralph Waldo Emerson in his Divinity School Address and in his essays believed that the young people of his day were diseased with the theological problems of original sin, the ideas of evil, predestination, and the like, good Calvinistic theological principles. But Emerson believed that these ideas represented the sickness of man. In his lecture on "The Times" (1841), Emerson declared that the terrors of sin had lost their force. He believed that grief could teach an individual nothing. He was sure that "good is positive, evil is merely privative, not absolute." He always affirmed optimism rather than pessimism.

Father Taylor, after hearing Emerson preach, declared that

Mr. Emerson is one of the sweetest creatures God ever made; there is a screw loose somewhere in the machinery, yet I cannot tell where it is, for I never heard it jar. He must go to heaven when he dies, for if he went to hell, the devil would not know what to do with him. But he knows no more of the religion of the New Testament than Balaam's ass did the principles of the Hebrew grammar.[16]

In *Moby-Dick*, we see that Melville had moved far from original Calvinism in his attitude about freedom of choice. *Moby-Dick* is a tragedy because there was free choice. No one had been forced to sail with the *Pequod*, especially with her peculiar captain. Captain Ahab was not predetermined, except by his own monomania, to chase the white whale. He could have turned away from the chase at any time. His monomania was not determined by God, and certainly not predetermined. It was his own stubbornness that caused his death and all of the crew except Ishmael. If Ahab had no other choice than to follow the white whale to his and the crew's ultimate destruction, it was not the will of God, but Ahab's will. This is the reason that this is a tragedy, because at any moment the tragedy could have been avoided, by 180 degrees right or left rudder. There was the possibility of choice. In the Calvinistic system everything is predetermined, which is a fairly discouraging prospect unless you know that you are one of the elect, and therefore are to be saved. There is no hint in *Moby-Dick* that God predetermined all of this, or there would be no story, no drama.

If Melville ever accepted the principles of orthodox Calvinism, it is evident in *Moby-Dick* that he had moved a long way from the religious teachings of his childhood. He has become at least an Arminian, and believed in free will. But he was still not in step with many of the Unitarians of his day who were strongly influenced by Ralph Waldo Emerson; who thought that mankind was getting better and better, and that evil was not real, but was only something to be overcome. It would only be after Melville had worked through all of his doubts and had learned to be more accepting of the fact that man cannot keep up with answers to his own questions, and that variety of belief is to be encouraged rather than creedalized, that he would turn again to the religion of his father and his wife and become a member of All Souls Unitarian Church. But leaving Calvinism was only the first step of his religious experience. He had other more painful steps yet to take before he could embrace any religious system at all.

Melville believed that he had conceived a masterpiece in the writing of *Moby-Dick*. We can say that the novel was a nineteenth century failure and a twentieth century comet. But it took the literary world a long time to agree that it was one of the most forceful novels ever written. The book was first published in London on 18 October 1851 as *The Whale* in three volumes, just four days before the Herman Melville's second child Stannwix was born at Pittsfield. The English reviews began to come in before the volume was published in the United States. *The Athenaeum* review was totally unsatisfactory so far as Melville's reputation was concerned. This review came out just a week after the publication of the book.

The reviewer termed it

> "an ill compounded mixture of romance and matter-of-fact . . . Our author must be henceforth numbered in the company of the incorrigibles who occasionally tantalize us with indications of genius, while they constantly summon us to endure monstrosities, carelessness, and other such harassing manifestations of bad taste as daring or disordered ingenuity can devise." It was further termed "as so much trash belonging to the worst school of Bedlam literature—since he seems so much unable to learn as disdainful of learning the craft of an artist."[17]

The Spectator called the book rhapsody run mad.[18] *John Bull*, on the other hand, praised the book, saying,

> Who would have looked for philosophy in whales, or for poetry in blubber . . . all things combine to raise *The Whale* far beyond the level of an ordinary work of fiction. It is not a mere tale of adventures, but a whole philosophy of life, that it unfolds.[19]

Moby-Dick was published in New York on 14 November 1851. Henry Wadsworth Longfellow wrote in his diary after spending all the evening reading the book: "Very wild, strange and interesting."[20] Evert Duyckinck wrote what would appear to be a rather critical review of *Moby-Dick* for one so close in friendship to the author. He found difficulty in understanding the book because a good tale was

> a most remarkable sea-dish, an intellectual chowder of romance, philosophy, natural history, fine writing, good feeling, bad sayings, but over which, in spite of the author himself, predominates his keen perceptive faculties, exhibited in keen narration.[21]

He believed that the character of Ahab was "too long drawn out." "If we had as much of Hamlet or Macbeth as Mr. Melville gives us of Ahab, we should be tired even of their sublime company."[22]

These are very strong powers with which Mr. Melville wrestles in this book. It would be a great glory to subdue them to the highest uses of fiction. It is still a great honor, among the crowd of successful mediocrities which throng our publishers counters, and know nothing of divine impulses, to be in the company of these nobler spirits on any terms.[23]

George Ripley caught the significance of the book when he wrote in Harper's *New Monthly Magazine*,

Beneath the whole story, the subtle and imaginative reader may perhaps find a pregnant allegory, intended to illustrate the mystery of human life. Certain it is that the rapid, pointed hints which are thrown out, with the keenness and velocity of a harpoon, penetrate deep into the heart of things, showing that the genius of the author for moral analysis is scarcely surpassed by the wizard power of description.[24]

Another London review in *The Literary Gazette* felt that after Mr. Melville had built such a fine literary reputation that he should "not waste his strength on such purposeless and unequal doings as these rambling volumes about spermaceti whales."[25]

These are but a few of the many comments which were launched at *Moby-Dick*, pro and con. Very few understood the meaning of the book and the spiritual implications of the struggle of good against evil as represented in the combat between Captain Ahab and the white whale.

These reviews are very important, for they made Melville draw even more within himself and to realize that he would write what he wanted to write whether the public liked it or not. In a way he wanted to be repudiated as a popular author, and the next two books, *Pierre* and *The Confidence Man* would complete the alienation of Herman Melville from even the human race itself. *Pierre* would be one of the most devastating books any man ever wrote about his own family, and *The Confidence Man* would purport to show that no human being could be trusted, and that things on the surface were never what was real.

C H A P T E R   S I X

DISILLUSIONMENT WITH HUMAN NATURE

Shortly before Herman Melville knew that *Moby-Dick* would be an economic failure, he assured Sophia Hawthorne that his next novel would be a "rural bowl of milk." But this is not the way that his next novel *Pierre* turned out at all. His new work was a bitter diatribe about people, and he is especially skeptical of human nature. The subtitle of *Pierre* was *The Ambiguities*. It is set in the rural setting that Melville had promised Mrs. Hawthorne, but it is the rural estate of the widowed Mrs. Glendinning who lives on a rather fine piece of real estate with her nineteen year old son Pierre.

Mrs. Glendinning had chosen a beautiful blond young woman, Lucy Tartan, to be Pierre's wife. But Pierre then discovered that a mysterious dark-haired girl, Isabel, was probably his illegitimate half-sister, sired by his father during his extensive travels as a young man. Pierre, in order to protect this girl, eloped with her, and although he intended to keep his relationship with her platonic, he soon found Isabel sexually tempting. Melville delicately insinuates that they were guilty of incest.

Pierre through all of this believed that he was doing the ethical thing. He believed himself to be a completely unselfish person who lived by a kind of celestial morality. The book in many ways is a satire on hypocrisy, a condemnation of the tastes of the period and what are conceived to be the social evils of the times. But as Gay Allen Wilson sums it up, "Pierre is betrayed by his mother, his cousin, and his own impulses to do good. His mother dies of wounded pride, Pierre, murders his cousin, and he, Isabel, and Lucy commit suicide."[1]

It was the writing of *Pierre*, written in a frenzied manner, and published in 1852 with its subsequent poor reception, that resulted in the nervous exhaustion from which Melville suffered in this period of his life. He was examined by Dr. Oliver Wendell Holmes, who assured Elizabeth that her husband was tired but not insane.

Dr. Henry A. Murray, a Harvard psychologist, was drawn to study the life of Herman Melville because his interest was whetted by *Pierre*. He wrote, "Pierre is the burning out of Melville's volcano."[2] But Murray agrees with Lewis Mumford's analysis that "Pierre is the performance of a depleted puppeteer."[3]

> In this book, Melville conceives of the annihilation of human character, the annihilation about which he later spoke to Nathaniel Hawthorne on his way to the Holy Land. In this novel Melville begins to see that the good and the evil conflict which he so magnificently depicted in *Moby-Dick* cannot be reconciled or blended.

As Murray wrote,

> He [Melville] discovers in due time a radical defect in every person who has appealed to him and begins hating what he has loved, though, unconsciously, he continues loving the object of his hate. Thus no whole-hearted embracing of anyone is possible, and the constructive tendency toward synthesis and integration is perpetually obstructed. This accounts for the majority of ambiguities (almost synonymous with ambivalences) in *Pierre*.[4]

But Henry Murray feels that it is futile to try to understand *Pierre* on a rational level of thought which so many critics have tried to do. He further wrote:

> It would also be well if critics were protected from the mistake of dealing with Melville's thought on a rational level as if he had arrived at his conclusions by logical inductions after an impartial survey of the universe; and from the mistake of supposing that Melville was searching for Truth as science defines it, and that his tragedy, therefore, was an intellectual one.[5]

We shall see later in *Clarel* that Herman Melville tries to solve the unsolvable problems of traditional philosophy with rational answers. In this, like Job, he does not succeed. But *Pierre* should not be conceived in this light. What we are witnessing here is a man fighting for spiritual survival, in which emotion plays a much stronger part in his deliberations than does the rationality of his mind. *Pierre* is simply not a novel for the rational mind. In fact, it is one of the first attempts at depth psychology in American literature. Hawthorne had attempted some of this, but Hawthorne's despair does not reach the level of emotional intensity as does Melville's. Americans today with little left in the way of religious belief, with a vision of God as some kind of a scientific blob like a distant corona, a world which is largely involved in solving technical problems, a world that has substituted the trivial for the depths, should find in *Pierre* a book not only difficult to read, but a book which stirs one to the depths and makes one wonder about the vitality and veracity of any human being.

Actually, *Pierre* is autobiographic, but in a peculiar sort of way. Henry Murray wrote that "Pierre is Oedipus-Romeo-Hamlet-Memnon-Christ-Ishmael-Orestes-Timon-Satan-Cain-Manfred, or, more shortly, an American Fallen and Crucified Angel."[6]

Most of the characters in the novel can be linked to people who were close to Melville in his life. His grandfather, General Peter Gansevoort, is certainly the model for General Glendinning; his mother, Maria Gansevoort, the model for Pierre's mother, Mrs. Mary Glendinning. His own father is obviously the model for Pierre's father. His wife Elizabeth may be the model for Lucy Tartan. There are other resemblances among the minor characters to people whom Herman Melville knew in real life. The sad thing is that he pictured these people whom he knew so well and were so close to him in such an unfavorable light, people in many cases without real character. Missing only are the people whom Melville knew in his four years at sea. In some ways he tried to hide the true identity of the characters, but in most cases they shine through very clearly.

What Melville was doing in writing *Pierre* was to go deeper and deeper into his own unconscious mind, and the results are a final disillusionment with human beings as not possibly being able to live on any plane that is exalted and noble. Yet this is not the final answer in Melville's spiritual autobiography, as we shall see. It is simply the low point emotionally in a very promising career than went awry so far as the public was concerned, but in the process produced a depth of understanding in novels that has been unsurpassed in American literature. Most American literary characters, with the possible exception of some of Hawthorne's characters, seem wooden and do not have the depths that we find in the characters in *Pierre*. The fact that we do not like these characters once we have met them and begin to understand them is not what is important. What is important is that these characters have been created and made alive, even if they are almost all disreputable.

> Perhaps the broadest generalization that can be made about Melville's different truths is that they are all culturally unacceptable. They are either shocking or depressing revelations about man's hidden self, or scathing condemnations of civilization, or offensive references to deity; or they are positive truths, in agreement with the Sermon on the Mount, which are ridiculous to men.[7]

"It was partially to avoid a barrage of gun shots that Melville concealed his truths in symbols, allegories, and myths in such a way that only a worthy reader can get at them,"[8] like the parables of Jesus.

In *The Confidence Man*, Herman Melville's next attempt at satire and a declaration of the bankruptcy of character of the human race, was published in April 1857. Melville had completed the book and sent it to the publisher, so that he was prepared to sail on 11 October 1856 to make a trip to visit Hawthorne in Liverpool in November, and then to continue on with his trip to Palestine. Although *The Confidence Man* had been published in April, Melville did not arrive back in New York until 20 May 1857, just in time to read the first unfavorable reviews of his book. If the world had rejected *Pierre*, it accepted *The Confidence Man* even less cordially.

In *The Confidence Man*, Melville again lays the scene aboard a ship. But in this novel it is a Mississippi steamboat rather than a United States man-of-war or a whaler. Melville tells the story as if it happened in a twenty-four-hour period as the steamboat makes stops at one town after another, and discharges and takes on new passengers. It takes place on the first of April, All Fool's Day, and just by coincidence the novel was published on 1 April 1857.

The Confidence Man is a novel in the sense that these are fictitious characters. But the main purpose of the book appears to be to satirize American culture as Melville saw it, as he had satirized world culture in *Mardi*. In *Pierre*, he had satirized and waylaid his own family. Actually what Melville is satirizing in *The Confidence Man* is the commonly held American opinion of this time that mankind is making some kind of evolutionary moral progress. No one among the *Fideles* passengers really believes this American myth so widely preached during the middle of the eighteenth century. *The Confidence Man* is the object of Melville's satire as he assumes one morally imperfect character after another. Melville is very aware of the inconsistencies of character in all human beings. People profess one thing and they do another, particularly if money is at stake. Money is the root of all of the sins of the various confidence men as they board the steamship and then leave it to be replaced by another phony.

Perhaps Lewis Mumford best sums it up.

> *The Confidence Man*, in his masquerade, represents all the sweetness and morality of the race, all that professes to see good in the human heart of evil, all the benign impulses to succor the poor and heal the sick, all that would place friendliness and natural intimacy above cold circumspection, that would make every alien soul a friend, and would place the needs of man above the safety of property.[9]

Mumford terms *The Confidence Man* a "palimpsest," which is a term usually referring to a Biblical document on parchment which has been erased and then a new text inscribed over the old, but the old text can still be read although seemingly erased. This means that beneath the story of the novel is another story, and that is the story of Melville's own life and thought, and his apparent belief in the destruction of human character. If we are basically concerned about the religion of Herman Melville, it is not the details of this fictitious trip on a Mississippi steamboat that ought to concern us as being important, but why Melville at this juncture of his life was so discouraged with human nature as to see what was normally conceived as many good things in this world as but a facade.

The unreality, according to Melville's thinking, was those generally accepted ideas; that charity for the poor was in itself good, for example. Yet Melville pointed out that behind every charitable endeavor there was some shyster looking out for his own interests, and those interests are certainly not those who might receive the charity. It is the kind of cynicism that one might develop in a modern scenario on television of adopting a child for twenty dollars a month, and the natural skepticism that many have, after so many bad experiences, that most of the money contributed does not go to the children at all, but to those who run the operation and the vast amounts of advertising that it takes to keep such an operation going with a constant stream of new contributors. People who in our time have seen television evangelists beg for money, and then turn multi-million dollar empires into cheating establishments have some basis upon which to be skeptical.

Melville's cynicism at this period in his life comes close to derangement, for on the Mississippi steamboat there is scarcely a character that has any redeeming character. As we would say in modern parlance, "They are all a bunch of crooks." We can ask if this is an overreaction. But it certainly shows a man who is despairing of the world, individuals in his own family in *Pierre*, and of most of the rest of humanity, especially the "do-gooders" in *The Confidence Man*.

Scholars appear to be generally agreed that this period in the middle 1850s was the low point of Herman Melville's spiritual and emotional life. In fact, when the Bellows-Samuel

Shaw correspondence was first published in 1975, many scholars were surprised that Mrs. Melville's desire to leave her husband came in 1867 rather than ten years earlier when he was writing these two books which are written in the depths of despair. The answer is that although he took a trip to the Promised Land, Herman Melville did not find the answers that he sought in the land of Palestine. Even treading in the shadows of the prophets and of Jesus, a visit to Nazareth did not destroy his doubts. He suffered through them through the long period of writing *Clarel*. Thus, Melville turns from his last novel to be publicly issued in his lifetime to the writing of poetry. But the content and the doubts and despair of his life continued at least until 1876 when *Clarel* finally saw the light of publication, almost two decades later.

There is little doubt that from the beginning *The Confidence Man* would not be a publishing success, for if there is one thing that people do not like it is to be called two-faced, dishonest, crafty, cunning, and immoral. The Pharisees didn't like to be called these names in the time of Jesus of Nazareth, and Jesus gave the word *Pharisee* a meaning so that it no longer, in most people's minds, refers to a sect of the Jewish religion, but to an entire attitude of mind in which character is meaningless and everyone is doing his own thing for his own profit at the expense of everyone else. Sometimes in reading the novel one gets the idea that the "Supreme Tempter" or Satan is occupying human flesh and is appearing constantly on the steamer. And, of course, the devil tries to make everything look moral and good. No nation ever fought a war for evil purposes, and no leader ever said to his people that he had deceived anyone. That comes out later in the general destruction of character that follows the dictates of power.

As R. W. B. Lewis writes in discussing *The Confidence Man*,

In short, the first and most accomplished of the confidence men in the novel is the author; and his first potential victim is the inattentive reader. The drastic aim of Melville's comedy of thought is to bring into question the sheer possibility of clear thinking itself—of 'knowing' anything. The aim is a sort of intellectual derangement, by arousing and deploying what Whitman called the terrible doubt of appearances, doubt every which way, doubt of the gold-buttoned gentleman's goodness . . . and then doubt of that doubt.[10]

Out of these particular and playful doubts, there gradually arise the more fateful ones, those which shake our foundations: doubt about goodness and beauty as existent realities anywhere in the world of man; doubt about the benevolence of God and nature, or for that matter about the cruelty and hostility of either; doubt, in the outcome the most desperate of all, about the remaining capacity for genuine friendship or charitable love between man and man.[11]

One is reminded a bit of the doubt of Rene Descartes with whose writings almost every college student begins a study of modern philosophical thought. Descartes doubted everything. He doubted man and God; and he doubted the existence of a real world. But in the end Descartes' doubts were less penetrating and less emotional than Melville's, for he soon discovered that he could not doubt that there was a doubter, himself. Melville is not trying to develop a system of philosophy, as was Descartes, but he was so disgusted with the whole human situation that he lashed out at his family in *Pierre*, and at the whole world and everyone in it in *The Confidence Man*. I would not begin an argument as to which of these two men was the greatest doubter, but there can be little argument with the thesis that Melville felt all of these evils more keenly than did the more cranial Descartes.

The long-term result of the publication failure of *The Confidence Man* was that Melville drew more and more within his own shell, felt that the world was against him and all that he stood for, so that he no longer spoke in positive terms (until *Billy Budd*), but was sour grapes on life itself, his own family, and all of the conniving human beings with whom he had contact. One can readily understand that he would be a difficult man to live with if he harbored constantly such modes of thought. And one can also understand why Elizabeth Melville might want to get away from a household which was brooded over by such blackness.

Raymond Weaver sums up the mood of this period by quoting an unnamed uncircumspect critic at the time of Melville's centenary in 1919:

From being a writer of stirring, vivid fiction, he became a dreamer, wrapping himself up in a vague kind of mysticism, that rendered his last few books such as *Pierre: or The Ambiguities* and *The Confidence Man: His Masquerade* quite incomprehensible, and certainly most uninteresting for the average reader.[12]

But we ought to add that this was a mysticism on the dark side and showed the escape that Melville made by denying the "rightness of almost everything." It was not a kind of invigorating mysticism which lifted the human spirit even in despair. We do not get that uplifting spirit even in the midst of tragedy until *Billy Budd*. Now we turn to Melville's rigorous attempts to answer the persistent questions of philosophy and religion which he tried to solve by a trip to the Holy Land.

Photo of Herman Melville taken in 1861 while he was living in Pittsfield.

List of Persons

in Congregation of

All Souls Church

New York.

Corrected up to January 1, 1885

To be kept in Communion table drawer, per order

Pres. of Board of Trustees.

Courtesy of the All Souls Archives.
Front page of Dr. Theodore Williams' "List of Persons in the Congregation of All Souls Church, New York, 1885."

Name	Address	
Murdock, U. A.	313 Fifth Ave	
Marquand, Jua. P.	13 W. 49	18 Wall
Melville, Herman	104 E. 26	
Mattison, Jos. 2 Mrs	91 Park Ave.	
Maynard, Effingham	286 Lexington	734 B'way
Merill, Edw. P.	145 W. 12	
Means, David M. 2 Mrs.	126 E. 28	
Mendleson, Mr.	209 W. 46	
Morrison, Robt Geo. S.	133 E. 21	
Mitchell, Mrs H. A.	Hotel Victoria	
Miller, Chas. P. 2 Mrs.	286 Lexington	24t
Mann, Mrs J. P.	969	
Miller, Geo. C. 2 Mrs	368 W. 106	
Matthews, S. A.	140 Madison	
McKeever, Lawrence	164 Lexington	128 Pearl
McDougall, Mrs.	Patchen N.	
Mr & Mrs Walter Mendelson	209 W 46	
Mr & Mrs Edwin Morse	W 57 & 9th Ave	
Mr & Mrs J H Morse	40 W 32	
Mrs Morrill	Fishkill	72 21
Mrs Wm & Mrs McKeever & Mrs		

Courtesy of All Souls Archives. List of Persons in Dr. Williams'
Membership Book which lists Herman Melville as a member.

ENTRANCE TO FIRST CONGREGATIONAL CHURCH,
BROADWAY · NEW YORK · MDCCCXLV ·

Courtesy of All Souls Archives. The Church of the Divine Unity on Broadway extending through to Crosby Street (between Prince and Spring Streets). The large Gothic structure could seat 1200 persons and was completed in 1845. Herman Melville rented a pew here before going to Pittsfield in 1860.

Courtesy of the All Souls Archives. All Souls Unitarian Church at Gramercy Park, Fourth Avenue (now named Park Avenue, South) and 20th Street. Completed in 1855. Because of its exterior it was often called "The Beefsteak Church." The Melvilles rented pews in this church from 1863 until Melville's death and Mrs. Melville rented a pew until her death in 1908.

Courtesy of All Souls Archives.
Dr. Theodore Chickering Williams.
Minister of All Souls from 1883 to 1897.

A·PATRIOT·LOVING·FREEDOM·INDIGNANT·AT·WRONG·

PRESIDENT·OF·THE·VNITED·STATES
SANITARY·COMMISSION·FROM

1861 To 1878

·HENRY·WHITNEY·BELLoWS·D·D·
·BoRN·IN·BoSToN·JVlIE·11ᵀᴴ·1814·
·DIED·IN·NEW·YoRK·JANVARY·30ᵗʰ·1882·

Courtesy of the All Souls Archives. The Augustus Saint-Gaudens bas-relief of Dr. Henry Whitney Bellows. Installed in the church in 1886.

C H A P T E R   S E V E N
THE DEPTHS OF SKEPTICISM
A N D   C L A R E L

After the publication and failure of *The Confidence Man*, the Melville and Gansevoort families were frightened that Herman was lapsing into some form of insanity. He had published *Pierre* in 1852, *Israel Potter* in 1855, and fifteen short stories. These included "Bartelby the Scrivener," which was published in Harper's *Monthly Magazine* in two installments for which Melville received eighty-five dollars. Successively he published "The Encantadas," "The Tartarus of Maids," "I and My Chimney," and "The Piazza Tales." In addition, his novel *Israel Potter* appeared in Putnams Magazine, and then was published as a book. But his backlog of books were all destroyed by a fire at Harpers on 10 December 1854, and thus his hopes of continued income from later sales evaporated. So Melville was desperate for money. *The Confidence Man* was published in 1857, and it was the last novel published in his lifetime. *Billy Budd* was not published until many years after Melville's death in 1891.

In April 1854, Melville submitted a story which indicated his attitude towards organized religion in his time. He wanted to worship in a church, but he felt like an outsider. He submitted this short story to Putnams. It was titled "Two Temples." The next month George Briggs Putnam rejected his work. But since out of all of his short stories this one tells us the most about his inner feelings about organized religion, we will eventually dwell at some length on it.

All of this writing during the middle and later part of the 1850s was an attempt to secure his position as a writer whose books would sell, but all of this energy expended left Melville physically and mentally exhausted. The family were of one mind that his future was not that of a novelist. He needed some sort of vacation. But Melville was broke. Judge Lemuel Shaw, his father-in-law responded, as usual, with a generous gift that enabled Herman to plan for a long trip.

Melville planned his trip as an extensive one. He first took a ship to England where he saw Nathaniel Hawthorne in Liverpool. Then he went to Egypt, the Holy Land, and Italy, and returned somewhat invigorated on 20 May 1857, just in time to read the rather unfavorable reviews of the book that had been published while he was away, *The Confidence Man.* Melville then tried to find other ways to support his family. He decided that he would tour the lecture circuit. He gave lectures on Roman statuary, classical mythology, and other similar topics. But his income from these lectures in no way secured him enough money to support his family. So in 1863, in the midst of the Civil War, he sold "Arrowhead" to his brother, Allan, and moved back to New York City. He bought a house at 104 East Twenty-sixth Street where he was to live the rest of his life. One hundred four East Twenty-sixth Street was near what is now called Park Avenue South, a fancier name for what he knew as Fourth Avenue.

The years in New York City are somewhat obscure. He did finally secure a position at the U.S. Customs House as an on-the-docks inspector of cargo. But the salary of four dollars per day, which was never increased in nineteen years, left the family to depend on the various legacies which various members of their families left to them in their wills. He had written what is, after the war-time works of Walt Whitman, some of the best poetry of the Civil War period. He published a set of poems called *Battle Pieces*, but again its reception was poor. Melville had visited several of the battlefields, and this volume of poetry was the result, published in 1866.

Work on the docks was tiring, and Melville evidently was in one of his more morose moods. Life with Herman at times became almost impossible.

The correspondence which the author found in the "Bellows Papers" in the Massachusetts Historical Society belong to this period. They revealed for the first time what was called the "smoking gun." Scholars had assumed that there were problems in the Melville household, but they never had any real evidence until these two letters were found and published. Mrs. Melville after Herman's death in 1891, did a rather thorough job in eliminating any material that might be incriminating to her husband's fame. But she did not have access to Henry Bellows' letters, for he had died in 1882, and the letters were secreted away from any public scrutiny.

One of the letters found in the "Bellows Papers" is from Elizabeth's half-brother, Samuel Shaw, a Boston lawyer who was doing some legal work for Henry Bellows, and to whom Bellows evidently wrote with the suggestion of "seemingly to kidnap against her will" (she was actually complying completely), and spirit her away to Boston to her brother's home, when Herman would be notified. Shaw, being a wise lawyer, did not think that this was very good advice. We do not know whose idea the kidnapping was, Bellows or Elizabeth's. Whoever thought it up, Bellows evidently wrote to Shaw with the suggestion, and the letter which was found was by Samuel Shaw, and was his reply to Bellows' letter. Bellows' letter to Samuel Shaw is not known to exist.

The second letter that was found was from Mrs. Melville to her minister, Dr. Bellows, who had left for a sabbatical in Europe, thanking him for all of his help in her problems.

But during this year of 1867, the times were very bad for the family, and finally in September the Melville's oldest child, Malcolm, died of a gunshot wound, either accidental or self-inflicted. The cause was never settled except legally, although legally it was called suicide. This brought the family to new depths of despair. But the discovery of this letter did prove one thing. It proved that it was trouble in the family that had caused Malcolm's suicide, and not that Malcolm's suicide caused the problems in which the family was mired.

But even during this period and the years which followed were in many ways the most satisfying times for Herman Melville. The family began to think that he was back to his normal self. He seemed to have risen out of the deepest depths of his despair. Melville was carefully writing his long poem *Clarel*, and seemingly enjoying the writing of poetry.

It took Melville almost twenty years to write his poem. He had left for the Holy Land in 1857, and *Clarel* was not published until 1876. Thus, there is a period of nineteen years when about the only evidence we have of Melville's thinking is contained in *Clarel*. Like so many of his novels, *Clarel* is largely autobiographical.

This poem has suffered the most oblivion of any of his writings. Its very length precludes a casual reading, for it contains eighteen thousand lines in iambic tetrameter, not a usual meter for such a poem. And reading it is not easy going, for some have said that after reading three pages of *Clarel* at night after one goes to bed, one is certain to have a deep and peaceful sleep. It wasn't until the 1940s that critics began to look at *Clarel* again.

Walter E. Bezanson, noted Melville scholar, has written about *Clarel*:

> There are few works of Anglo-American literature which rival *Clarel* as a rendering of the spiritual exigencies of the late Victorian era. The poem is an intricate documentation of a major crisis in Western civilization—the apparent smash-up of revealed religion in an age of Darwin. To the lyric despair of Tennyson, Arnold and Clough, and to the softer distress of Lowell and Longfellow, Melville added not only a more sizable lamentation, but this in-close fictional study of what the crisis meant to various representative men. He did his utmost to project more than his own spiritual dilemma. His effort to cope with the major tensions of the age makes *Clarel* a historical document almost of the first order.[1]

To accomplish his purpose of writing a book about the Holy Land, Melville conceived of his hero Clarel as a student of divinity who had dropped out of seminary because of his skepticism and loss of faith. In a very real sense, Clarel is Melville, continually asking all sorts of religious and theological questions. When Herman had visited Nathaniel Hawthorne in Liverpool at the beginning of his trip, Hawthorne had written that Melville was besieged in his mind with all kinds of unanswerable theological questions. Perhaps his mind was a bit like what at one time was a description of Union Theological Seminary in New York City. It was said that "it was a place which gave answers to all of the theological questions that no one was asking." But Melville in this period of skepticism was asking all of the questions, and he was not getting final answers because he could not accept the premises upon which the final answers must be built; revelation, holy writ, or church authority. Melville was a man to whom final answers that were accepted from others were not satisfactory. He had to think them through for himself.

In writing *Clarel* over a period of almost two decades, in the latter part of his life, Melville was trying to find the answers. And he did not find them for himself, and his search ended in skepticism. In *Clarel* a lot of people whom the divinity student meets in his ten-day journey in the Holy Land give him answers. Clarel is like Job whose friends tried to explain to him why he suffered. And Job would accept no answer from his friends. Clarel accepts no answers for himself from all of those people whom he meets on his journey.

It is not the author's purpose to go through all of the intricacies of *Clarel*. One should dip into the book to catch the spirit of what Melville was trying to do. Suffice it to say that *Clarel* is the final gasp of intellectualism about religion and theology, in many places so obscure as to belie understanding. Much is left to mystery.

The scene is laid in the Holy Land. Clarel has arrived in Jerusalem to begin his travels. He meets some interesting people, but almost immediately he falls in love with a young Jewish girl, Ruth, whose father, an immigrant from America to Palestine, is killed by hostile Arab raiders. A period of mourning follows, and according to Jewish custom, Clarel is not allowed to see Ruth. So Clarel sets out with a group of travelers on horseback. They embark upon a journey that takes them from Jerusalem to the wilderness of the Dead Sea and Jericho. Then they travel up a wadi to the Greek Orthodox monastery at Mar Saba. From there they travel to

Bethlehem, and then back to Jerusalem, where Clarel learns that Ruth has died of grief in his absence.

As in his novels so now in Melville's poetry, Ruth is a shadowy figure. Melville was not adept at making the women of his novels and poems into real people. But at least Ruth is a good feminine character, like Fayaway in *Typee*, not like Mrs. Glendenning in *Pierre*. But the character of Ruth is never worked out. The love theme is not sustained and only appears from time to time. This is the simple story of *Clarel*. But it not the story that is important to Melville, and even the journey is not significant, although it gave him a chance to use his knowledge of this area where he had traveled in 1857. It is the playing out of ideas, religious, philosophical, and theological, and finding no answers, that is the purpose and meaning of *Clarel*.

Many of those who have studied *Clarel* have believed that this was the final state of Melville's thinking about matters religious, that he died fifteen years after *Clarel* was published still skeptical, having found no personal philosophy that was satisfactory to him or to his searching mind, and that he died a skeptic.

But all of those who have studied the late years of Herman Melville's life before 1874, have not known the fact that some nine years after *Clarel* was published, Melville had made enough peace with his own mind and soul to go to his minister, Theodore Chickering Williams of All Souls Unitarian Church, and where the family had rented a pew off and on since 1850, and to ask to be entered on the books as a member of the church. The path had been from the Calvinism of his youth, to disillusionment with most everything in life, human and divine, with the Christian missionaries in the South Seas, disillusionment with his family in *Pierre*, and finally the utter skepticism of *Clarel* about finding rational answers to all of the problems of existence. Finally in his last years he found peace in Unitarianism, the religion of his father's side of the family. But we shall discuss this at length in the final chapter. Suffice it to say at this juncture that Melville did not rest eternally in his skepticism.

n.b.

Yet even in *Clarel* there are some signs that Melville was seeking for a new faith. In the epilogue in *Clarel*, which perhaps he wrote last, one begins to sense his seeking of a different end to his thinking than the skepticism of a Clarel. He mentions "The sign of the cross—the spirit above the dust." And his final advice to Clarel, the skeptical divinity student, is this:

cf.

> Then keep thy heart, though yet but ill-resigned-
> Clarel, thy heart, the issues there but mind;
> That like the crocus budding through the snow-
> That like the swimmer rising from the deep-
> That like a burning secret which doth go
> Even from the bosom that would hoard and keep;
> Emerge thou mayest from the last whelming sea,
> And prove that death but routs life into victory.[2]

CHAPTER EIGHT

THE LAST YEARS, THE CHRIST FIGURE,
AND *BILLY BUDD*

"The manuscript of *Billy Budd* as Melville left it at his death in 1891 may be most accurately described as a semi-final draft, not a final fair copy ready for publication." It was an unfinished work. In its writing it passed through several distinct stages. In each of these phases the original focus was radically changed. The literary world owes Harrison Hayford and Merton M. Sealts Jr. acclaim for taking the various manuscripts and making the book into a clean copy ready for the printer. Melville started work on it perhaps as early as 1886 when he retired from the U.S. Custom's House. Hayford and Sealts declare that in the early stage Billy was the only main character. But then Claggart came into the novel, and then Captain Vere.

The basic story of *Billy Budd; Sailor* is well known. Billy Budd is impressed into the British navy during wartime. The scene is laid in 1798. On the warship he is very popular, for he is an ideal sailor. He gets along well with everyone except Claggart, the Master-at-Arms. Because of his jealousy of this popularity Claggart looks for something that he can pin on Billy. Finally he begins to believe that Billy is trying to organize a mutiny among the crew. Claggart goes to Captain Vere with his story.

Billy is called before the captain, and Claggart repeats his charges. Billy has one impediment; he stutters, and when Claggart accuses him, he is unable to say anything. But almost involuntarily his fist shoots out and strikes Claggart on the temple, accidentally killing him. Now Billy is accused by Captain Vere of striking a superior officer and for that offense the punishment in the British Navy is death. So Billy Budd is hung on the yardarm early the next morning.

It is the often told tale of the good but misunderstood man who goes to his death because he does not fit into the social norms—in this case, "Navy Regulations"—of those around him. This is the simple story, but as in all of Melville's writing, the novel is filled with allegory and indecipherable overtones, so that there are almost as many interpretations as to what the novel means as there are interpreters. Melville tells the story simply and straightforwardly. It is such a simple story that the book is often given to young teenagers to read, although the vocabulary is often considered quite difficult.

The period from the publication of *Clarel* in 1876 until Melville's death in 1891 is often looked upon as a dreary time in Melville's life. Raymond Weaver in his early biography of Melville, *Herman Melville: Mariner and Mystic*, published in 1921, calls this period "the Long Quietus." He also called the period of the move from Pittsfield in 1863 until Melville's death, "perhaps the darkest years in Melville's life." Weaver also terms *Billy Budd* "not distinguished . . . the orphic sententiousness is gone it's true. But gone also is the brisk lucidity, the sparkle, the verve. Only the disillusion abided with him to the last."[1]

Raymond Weaver had a difficult time filling these last pages of his biography of Herman Melville, for at that time there were few facts known about Melville's later years.

William Ellery Sedgwick in one of the earlier analyses of Herman Melville (1944), gives us a very different picture of the meaning of *Billy Budd*. Sedgwick believes that Melville can be compared to Shakespeare in his handling of tragedy.

"Once more the parallel between Melville and Shakespeare comes to the front. For *Billy Budd* stands in the same light as *Moby-Dick* and *Pierre* that Shakespeare's last plays—*Pericles, The Winter's Tale, Cymbeline,* and *The Tempest*—stand to the great tragedies. Of Shakespeare in these plays it is often said, as of Melville in *Billy Budd*, that he came to accept life. Sedgwick goes on to say that acceptance is not quite the right word because it is too blunt and passive. Sedgwick writes that rather than acceptance he would "use the combination of words, recognition, restoration, and return."[2]

Sedgwick continues:

> The final and ever so poignant flowering of Herman Melville, which is the element of present lyrical experience in *Billy Budd*, is the same essentially as Shakespeare's in his last play . . . It is obvious on second sight that there was more to this than willful or sentimental retrospection. The same enchantment of life which he had thrilled to in his first book, he has returned to by force of insight in his last, and recognized it anew. Now, however, it is not localized; it is not identified as lying afar off.[3]

Sedgwick concludes his study with these words:

> Such is the force of Melville's final insight that the innocence and loveliness and joy of life is represented on board a man-of-war, Melville's own symbol for the world in its most opposite aspects to life as he had identified it with the Typee valley. True, this innocence suffers a shameful death at the hands of this man-of-war world. Yet, in Billy's life there is more promise of salvation for the world than there is of damnation in his death. And Melville has partaken of its salvation. His intellectual passion spent, and illuminated by his insight of a mind which by accepting its limitations has transcended them and has found within itself, at its own mysterious center, a calm not to be found elsewhere, Melville has been restored to the radiant visage of life, whose shining secret is, it has its salvation in its own keeping.[4]

In his life of Melville, Edwin Haviland Miller, gives an entirely different interpretation, and says of *Billy Budd*:

> In the course of the evolution of the tale into its seemingly final form it became a love story, the familiar love story in Melville's books . . . Melville fell in love with his artifact, or, perhaps more accurately, renewed and restated his love for the icon of the handsome youth, the wish fulfillment of his narcissistic needs and imagination. If in the tale Vere and Claggart are in love with Billy, the one as "father," and the other as rival, their love is extended by that of the author. Billy is truly Melville's love-child, the recipient of pent-up affections and feelings which in life he could, sadly, give to no one, except perhaps to Nathaniel Hawthorne.[5]

Miller continues this Freudian analysis of the hero:

> Billy incorporates both sexes—the most magnificent hermaphrodite of all Melville's hermaphrodites. The face is of "feminine purity of natural complexion," . . . although the muscular body was subtly modified by another and pervasive quality.[6]

If one is going to analyze *Billy Budd* and Melville in Freudian terms I suppose that Edwin Miller does it as well as anyone. The real question is whether applying these terms is a true process or only one that is fashionable, and scarcely based upon facts, explaining almost any mystery in terms of "mother" and "father," etc. It results in an interesting conclusion which Miller draws:

> Billy's fate confirms that the hermaphroditic icon is life-denying, or more kindly, life-evading, Billy and all the handsome sailors want out from adult heterosexuality; they want to be neither husbands nor fathers . . . From the beginning to his last work, Melville wanted to transcend a sexuality which he found anxiety-producing . . . Billy in death leaps the vexed human state.[7]

Is this an example of adopting a theory and then fitting the author and the characters of his novels to fit into that theory? I think that it may very well be. Of course, in 1975 when Dr. Miller wrote his book, the fact that Herman Melville had joined a Unitarian church around 1885 was not well known, although Miller must have sensed some Unitarian connections. In one of the last paragraphs in his "Epilogue" he writes: "A short service was held on September 30 at 104 East 26th Street. The Reverend Mr. Theodore C. Williams of All Souls Church officiated."[8] Or perhaps, like the view of many other scholars, the name "All Souls" did not connote a Unitarian but perhaps an Episcopalian church. If Miller had known this fact about Melville's Unitarianism, his attitude about the final meaning of *Billy Budd* might have been less Freudian and more humanistic.

In his study of Melville and his humanism, Ray B. Browne comes to an entirely different analysis which is sociological rather than Freudian. Browne believes that *Billy Budd* is second in greatness only to *Moby-Dick*. He calls it "one of the most provocative and disturbing books ever written."[9] Browne writes:

[Melville's] conclusion about life was a firm affirmation. *Billy Budd* demonstrates that Melville ended life with the same attitude he had held all of his mature years. He realized that in this man-of-war world in which Christ cannot exist, or has been extracted by God or expelled by man, the only hope of and for man is mankind itself . . . The feeling may be one of quiet acceptance but not at all one of resignation. There is no sniveling, no regret, no remorse. If life is that way, he seems to say, so be it. One must walk with dignity and with hope.[10]

Then Browne shows his political or sociological emphasis: This hope lies in *Billy Budd*, as with Melville's other works, with the common man, the people, with democracy, with the heroic men who all together make up mankind.[11]

In Melville's novel *Billy Budd*, Browne asserts that the common man is really a superman. The heroic sailor image is everywhere apparent. Here is this illiterate who could not read, but he could sing. He had a fatal flaw of stuttering which was his downfall. Just one asset short of "superman."

Then Browne speaks of the political characteristics of the novel:

On a strictly political level *Billy Budd* is a search for the best form of government—autocratic versus democratic—a question Melville worries about all of his mature life, especially during the writing of *Clarel*.[12]

The novel becomes, then, a study in the conflict between these opposing ideologies. In this context the struggle is not between Claggart and Budd, but between Captain Vere as spokesman and apologist for authority . . . and Billy, who is on this level, Melville takes great pains to point out, representative of the common ordinary sailor, the voice of the people in their insistence on their rights.[13]

Browne believes that:

Most important is Melville's affirmation of humanism, pictured through Billy. The chaplain, though serving Mars as well as God, recognizes that Billy though a 'barbarian' is best prepared to face the hereafter . . . Later the theme of the brotherhood of man and man's longing for this brotherhood—humanism—is taken up and reemphasized . . . in *Billy Budd* the singer of the ballad, ending the account with the immortal version of the whole affair, wants above all to "shake a friendly hand ere I sink."[14]

In his recent book, Paul McCarthy is concerned with madness and insanity in Melville's fiction. Melville himself at times came very close to the madness that had taken his father's life. The family worried when he began to brood, particularly in 1857 when he saw his doctor to see if he was actually insane.

Cf.
Melville was well aware that Elizabeth usually worried about his mental condition and that others in the family had at least occasional doubts about his balance or stability. He had his own doubts. During trying circumstances at home or at work, he likely felt once again the old fear of the twisted mind, of inherited insanity.[15]

In addition to these inner feelings that he may have had about his own sanity, there was a constant series of deaths in the family. Stannwix, the only surviving son, died at age thirty-five in San Francisco. And his death could only have stirred the family emotions once again about the mysterious death of Malcolm. How good a father Melville was to his children we do not really know, but Malcolm committed suicide, and Stannwix never did get well adjusted to life and died early.

"In *Billy Budd, Sailor*, (Melville) tried to resolve the ironies and complexities of the father-son relationships that in actual life more often than not he handled ineptly."[16]

McCarthy states that:

N.D.
Three figures aboard the *Bellipotent* [this name of the warship also appears in the original manuscript] disclose some degree of mental aberration. Master-at-Arms Claggart, the unnamed surgeon, and Captain Vere reveal that Melville's knowledge of insanity had not diminished after *Clarel* (1876), although his interest in scientific explanations had apparently abated."[17]

McCarthy also believes that Melville went his father one or two better: He did not succumb to mental illness or to despair, and he did survive. He managed to cope with many problems, including fears of the twisted mind.

Cf The bottom line for Melville may have been expressed in *Billy Budd, Sailor*: "Truth uncompromisingly told will always have its ragged edges." Melville was deeply aware of the ragged edges and insidious encroachments of insanity, just as he was deeply aware of the great difficulties of writing about them and of convincing readers to believe what he had written. His perseverance somehow paid off. Melville's fiction illustrates the depth of his understanding of abnormality and the integrity, determination, and art with which he expressed that understanding.[18]

Lewis Mumford, in one of the earliest interpretations of the late years of Herman Melville finds:

That Peace and oneness with Nature . . . came at last to Melville in the closing years of his life. He had renounced much; but he had gained much. What is life? the king in *Mardi* had asked the philosopher; and the philosopher had said: That question is more final than any answer. After much doubt, exacerbation, searching, after a long weary pilgrimage through books and lands, and not a little intercourse with men. Melville was now back to the view of his youth: he now accepted its finality. What power and heroic defiance had not accomplished, love, which has its philosophic equivalent in the desire to merge oneself with the universe and surrender to it, and accept its purposes, as one accepts the desires and whims and aims of one's beloved—love has achieved this.[19]

Mumford continues:

[Melville recognized] that intelligence, power, virtue, are not prime movers themselves, but derivative mechanisms that transmit and utilize the energy of life. If one spurn that energy and deny its sources, one's dreams are futile and one's hopes empty: but when one accepts life itself as the primary fact, then the dying year brings no grief, and all that fades and decays is but a pledge of what shall again, one day, live and flourish: the very universe itself, and space and time, are but modes of being, no more eternal than the senses that react to them and project them upon the forms that make them useful and significant to man. Whatever be the ultimate nature of things, the universe man conceives is still held together at his own centre: its significance is part and parcel of his own . . . The seed that in its growth pries open the rock has more power than the inert and brutal elements that oppose it, and there is a seed in man whose growth cannot be denied, a seed that binds him to all life, and causes him to direct his energies, despite frustrations, despite warring elements in his own being, towards a fuller existence marked by love and understanding.[20]

Lewis Mumford then draws this conclusion:

Melville had faced this colourless, unintegrated, primal world that underlies and antedates that which we know through our senses, our feelings, our experiences: he had touched the bare, unkind beginning of things, that chaos which existed when darkness reigned over the face of the waters, and only Moby-Dick had stirred in the deep: he had beheld the white unrefracted truth which exists before it passes through man's being and is broken up into colours of art and thought and custom and ritual and organized society . . . At last he escaped from that bleak ultimate revelation, and, participating in the ancient cycle of life, he found his own life renewed once more.[21]

This hints at the ultimate religious experience, and often it comes, as it did in Melville's life, after a lifetime of doubting and despair, despair of man's nature, and even of God's nature. But eventually it comes back to an experience of the Oneness of things, in which all dualities are absorbed. In the East it has been expressed in different words than in the West, but it is a description of the ultimate awareness that man has of his dependency upon something Other than himself, in this case called not God but Nature. But they become synonymous.

It is well in studying Herman Melville to keep many books at one's side to see just how varied the interpretations can be. In looking at the various ways in which Melville scholars have interpreted *Billy Budd* we have seen a whole panorama of interpretations. The reader might well ask: "Is another interpretation needed?" Probably not, if there were no new facts upon which to base an interpretation. Facts about Melville's last years have been notoriously difficult to find, and in short supply. So much was destroyed or lost. So when a new fact is unearthed the more sensitive Melville scholars rejoice, for here is a fact, not another theory upon which to base some conclusions.

That is the reason most of the scholars were overjoyed when the author stumbled upon the Bellows-Shaw correspondence. Here were some new facts. There were some real problems in the Melville household so serious that Elizabeth went to her minister, Dr. Bellows, with the suggestion of a feigned kidnapping. The scholars welcomed this new fact for it fit into their suspicions that there was a deep-seated problem between Herman and Elizabeth.

But it has seemed to the author that the scholars should have equally welcomed the other new fact; that in his later years Herman Melville joined the All Souls Unitarian Church. On this matter there has been almost complete silence. Either this new fact does not fit into conveniently held theories, or else the scholars do not understand the Unitarian movement in the 1880s.

The discovery of this new fact about Melville's church membership makes these last years not the least significant but perhaps the most significant years of Melville's life. *Billy Budd* is now considered almost universally to be one of the great short novels in the English language, now that the surviving manuscripts have been collated by Melville scholars, and the book published. *Two Discoveries About Herman Melville* published by the Massachusetts Historical Society *Proceedings*, showed not only that in 1867 there was great disillusionment in the Melville family with the kidnapping proposed so that Elizabeth could get away from a man very difficult to live with. The article also told the world for the first time that Herman Melville in his later years had voluntarily joined a church. Furthermore it was, unthinkably, a Unitarian Church, the All Souls Unitarian Church in New York City, which was presided over by Dr. Henry Bellows until his death in 1882, and then by his successor, Theodore Chickering Williams, from 1883 until 1896. The author is very surprised that Melville scholars did not perhaps think that this revelation of Unitarian church membership was even more important than the revelation of the family troubles. It was usually assumed that Melville never joined a church, and particularly not in his later years.

Sometime between 1883 and 1885, Herman Melville went to see Dr. Williams and asked his minister that his name be entered upon the rolls as a *member* of the church. Dr. Williams wrote his name in a small book still in the possession of the church which listed his name, and listed his address as "104 East 26th Street." So there could be no question that this Herman Melville was *the* Herman Melville. As was suggested in the Preface, very few have even commented on the fact that Melville joined a Unitarian church. The proof is recorded for anyone to see published in a small booklet by the Melville Society.[22]

There are many ways that one can handle this new fact. Some of the Melville scholars discount the evidence because it does not fit into past theories about Melville's formal religious affiliation which was assumed to be non-existent. Scholars who discount this are apt to say, "Well, Herman went to church occasionally to please Lizzie." But that is precisely wrong. When the family first rented a pew in Dr. Bellows church in 1850 just before leaving New York City for Pittsfield that might have been true. It might also have been true after the return from Pittsfield in 1863 when the family again rented a pew. Sometimes the pew was entered in the church books as rented by Herman and sometimes by Elizabeth Melville.

To clear up this matter we must understand that in churches in the New England Congregational and Unitarian traditions, a tradition at All Souls, buying or renting a pew and becoming a member of the church were two very different things. There was a great deal of overlap, and most of the pew-holders and renters were actually members of the church. But renting or owning a pew did not automatically make one a member of the church. Those who say that Melville simply wanted to please his wife by going to church fail to understand that under the bylaws of All Souls Church anyone who wanted to become a member of the church had to signify this intent to the minister of the church.[23]

The author believes that one has to take seriously Melville's membership in the church. It was not a casual thing. The family had rented pews in the church for many years. Usually the pew was one of the least expensive pews in the church, and the Melvilles never had the substance to *buy* a pew. But joining the church was a much more serious spiritual endeavor than the mere renting of a pew, so that when the family wanted to go to church they had a place to sit.

Melville's joining the church, I believe, also represents a resolution of many of the doubts that had plagued him all of his life, and which received their final frustration in *Clarel*. Lawrance Thompson wrote a book titled *Melville's Quarrel with God*.[24] It would appear now that perhaps these last years of Melville's life could be called Melville's reconciliation with God, and the end of his quarrel with God, for it was during these later years that he joined the Unitarian Church and that he wrote *Billy Budd*. It appears that in writing *Billy Budd* he began to conceive of his own frustrated life in an ideal way, that he identified himself with Billy Budd and with the figure of the Christ crucified on the yardarm, and that in a rather unusual way he found peace within himself. After all of the struggles of his lifetime, his birth into and upbringing in a conservative Calvinistic Protestant sect, his disillusionment with the Christian missionaries in the South Seas, his adoption of a kind of dualism of right against wrong or light against darkness in *Moby-Dick*, his wrestling with family disillusionment in *Pierre*, his searching out of answers to many of the deeper philosophical and theological problems in *Clarel*, he finally found his answer in the Christ figure of Billy Budd.

If Melville joined a Unitarian church, exactly what did Unitarian churches believe in his time, and especially what was the primary theology and philosophy of All Souls Unitarian Church in New York City. One can make general statements about Unitarianism in America in this period, but each Unitarian Church was an entity within itself, and they did not necessarily resemble each other in basic beliefs.[25]

In Bellows' time the newly propounded theory of evolution by Charles Darwin and others, strongly affected theological thinking. There had been a tendency to think after Emerson's "Divinity School Address" that there was a kind of unreality about evil. Evil was lack of good just as darkness was lack of light. Many Unitarian preachers waxed eloquent with optimism about the future of mankind, for it was conceived that evolution applied to human history, and that mankind would get better and better. Dr. Bellows must have driven Herman Melville mad preaching this sort of doctrine, for Herman Melville did not believe that evil was simply illusory. He believed that evil was very real.

In Unitarian churches of that time there usually was a rather broad covenant, and every member of the church was encouraged to fill in the details of his belief. There were bound to be vast differences, and the genius of the Unitarian faith was that these differences were recognized and more than tolerated; they were encouraged. So it was perfectly possible for a parishioner to completely disagree on vital theological matters with not only his minister but with many other parishioners. This was truly diversity within a worshipping unity. If there were a thousand members of Dr. Bellows' church, there were probably a thousand different concepts of God, the Christ figure, and all of the matters of theology that people believed were relevant.

When Theodore Chickering Williams arrived at All Souls as a brilliant young Harvard University and Harvard Divinity School graduate, a language enthusiast for the classics, and a class orator, the congregation expected that they had found another young Bellows. In this they were to be keenly disappointed, for Williams was essentially a poet at heart. He published several volumes of poetry during his lifetime, but more importantly he wrote many words to hymns which were used for many years in the Unitarian churches in America. A few have survived usage for a century or more. He and his wife published a hymnal which contained many of his words to hymn tunes, and other hymns. It was used as a supplemental hymnbook in many Unitarian churches.

Having studied these two minister's writings and the writings of Melville, I thoroughly believe that Herman Melville would have found Williams far more compatible to his way of thinking than he would have to those ideas of Henry Bellows who was an activist of another stamp. Herman Melville in addition to working on *Billy Budd* in his later years was also writing poetry, and two small volumes of these poems were published privately in very small editions of only twenty-five copies.

So Herman Melville may have found in his church some new meaning after Bellows' death and the coming of Dr. Williams. They were, I believe, kindred souls. It was fairly easy in spite of a natural reluctance for him to approach Williams and to join the church. It would have been well nigh impossible for him to have approached Bellows to join the church. So this was a significant event in his later life.

Returning again to Melville's amazing novelette, there have been many interpretations of the meaning of *Billy Budd*, but essentially the story is one of a good but misunderstood young sailor being hung on the yardarm because he struck a superior officer. Somehow, one cannot help but compare the figure of Billy Budd with the Christ figure on the cross. From the Unitarian point of view, Jesus of Nazareth was one in a great line of prophets. He had no special divinity. Unitarians were fairly much in agreement on this idea during Melville's later years, except for a few very conservative ministers. From a humanistic point of view, skipping the orthodox theological niceties, Jesus was crucified because he was misunderstood by men, both the Romans and the Jews. The people thought that he wanted to be a worldly king, a son of David (the reason that the genealogies trace his ancestry back to David in the Gospels of Matthew and Luke).

But Jesus said that his kingdom was not of this world. His was a spiritual world, entrance to which was to be gained by a very simple formula— be kind to your neighbor, and if he is hungry feed him, and if he's thirsty, give him drink. Jesus himself gave no theological formulae for gaining salvation except the admonition for one to treat others as one's self would like to be treated. The Jews misunderstood him because he disobeyed Jewish law, just as Billy Budd had to be killed because he had struck a superior officer, and that crime was punishable by death. Even Captain Vere did not want to put Billy Budd to death, but his hands were literally tied by "Navy Regulations."

In the original version of the poem *"Billy in the Darbies"* which ends the novel, Melville made a more direct reference to the Christ figure. Hayford and Sealts write of this early version.

N. 3,

> Very good of him, Ay, so long to stay
> And down on his marrow bone here to pray
> For the likes of me. Nor bad his story,
> The Good Being hung and gone to glory.

In the final version we read:

> Good of the chaplain to enter Lone Bay
> And down on his marrow bones here and pray
> For the like just o'me, Billy Budd.[26]

Somehow in his mind, it seems to me, Herman Melville began to associate himself with the idea that he was one who had been spurned of men because he did not want to write about south sea maidens any longer, but wanted to grapple with the deeper problems of existence, many of which in many circles were taboo subjects for discussion.

The final poem which concludes this prose work of *Billy Budd* is called *Billy in the Darbies*, which means Billy in chains. The chaplain comes in to pray for Billy, but Billy is more interested in the works of Nature that he sees around him. "But look: Through the port comes the moonshine astray! It tips the guard's cutlass and silvers this nook." In the poem Billy doesn't want to be hoisted to the yardarm on an empty stomach.

> "They give me a nibble—bit o' biscuit ere I go.
> Sure a messmate will reach me the last parting cup."

These lines might suggest just a simple biscuit and a cup of something to drink. But they might suggest a last sacrament of bread and wine before Billy dies. We do not know what Melville meant by these lines, but they could imply that they have something to do with the Christ figure and the Last Supper. The communion service celebrated in All Souls Unitarian Church was "in the spirit of the Last Supper." It had no magical meaning. There was no transubstantiation or con-substantiation of the elements into the actual body and blood of Christ. It was a simple memorial service that linked the worshiper with God through partaking of the bread and the wine as a celebration of the life and death of Jesus Christ.

> But me they'll lash in hammock, drop me deep.
> Fathoms down, fathoms down, how I'll dream fast asleep.
> I feel it stealing now. Sentry are you there?
> Just ease these darbies at the wrist,
> And roll me over fair!
> I am sleepy, and the oozy weeds about me twist.[27]

Melville was as nearly at peace within his own soul as it was possible for a man to be who was always asking the ultimate questions. He closed *Clarel* with words of hope. And then he wrote a simple story about a good sailor who was crucified by a cruel world whose laws were misbegotten, and whose values were askew. But in the simple being of Billy Budd lay the kernel of truth that Melville had sought and searched for all of his life.

C H A P T E R   N I N E

UNITARIANISM IN 1885:
ALL SOULS CHURCH

Now that we are presented with a new fact rather than a theory about Herman Melville—that he actually joined All Souls Unitarian Church in New York City around 1885—what difference does it mean in our interpretation of the spiritual odyssey of Herman Melville? Does it mean nothing at all, or is it a highly significant find that enables us to understand better his spiritual odyssey? I believe that it is most significant, and I will elucidate my reasons for thinking so.

It is a mistake to believe that all Unitarians in 1885 thought alike in many religious matters. As I wrote in the Preface, when I told a noted Unitarian scholar, the late James Luther Adams, that Melville had joined All Souls Church, he said that it was not surprising for Unitarianism by its very nature was not a monolithic set of beliefs, then or now. He remarked that it showed there were as many Unitarian beliefs in that century as there are today. It would be a mistake for us to attribute to Herman Melville many of the beliefs of his contemporary fellow Unitarians. Therefore, it is necessary to speak not only of Unitarianism in general but specifically as it related to All Souls Church in New York City. To me this makes all of the hours of research that I have spent in writing the three volume history of All Souls more worthwhile, because the study of the history of this church is more meaningful. It becomes not just the history of a particular parish, but the study of the history of a parish that nurtured one of America's greatest novelists, and his religious convictions.

Let us look at Unitarianism in general in the first instance and then more specifically at All Souls Church, and try to picture it as it was in 1885.

Unitarianism in many ways was a product of New England Congregational thinking. During the early part of the nineteenth century among the Congregational churches in New England, and especially in and around Boston, there arose what came to be called "The Unitarian Heresy." Many of the ministers of these churches began to speak more and more about their opposition to some of the doctrines of Calvinism. These ministers at that time had no desire to separate from their Congregational brethren who were more conservative. In fact, they made every effort to remain within the Congregational fold.

But Jedediah Morse, the settled minister in Charlestown, Massachusetts, and some of the more conservative Congregationalists were adamant that this new heresy should not creep into the Congregational churches. In a time of long sermons with much preparation required and when exchanging pulpits was an important custom among ministers, they did not open their pulpits to anyone who professed these "new" ideas. Open warfare was declared in 1815 when Morse characterized these thinkers as "Unitarians," a term that they themselves had been loathe to use. Morse used this term not as one of approbation but as one of derision. William Ellery Channing and other clergy of a more liberal theological persuasion decided to use the name "Unitarian" in a positive way. The name that Jedediah Morse had heaped upon them in derision, they turned into a positive belief. So from that date onward this group became "The Unitarians."

Many of these more liberal thinkers, such as Aaron Bancroft in Worcester, earlier had used the term "Arminian" to distinguish their beliefs from the Calvinistic determinists. Arminius, a Dutch theologian, disagreed with the Calvinists in the doctrine of original sin and determinism. Arminius stated that he believed man had free will and that everything was not determined by God in advance. Gradually these theological liberals who considered themselves Arminians took on this new name "Unitarian" even though it had some different theological implications than Arminianism. The term "Unitarian" expressed not so much an attitude towards God, for most Christians professed to believe in one God even though they postulated three persons in the Godhead, as it was the nature of Jesus that was primarily in question. Was Christ part of an Eternal Trinity, or had he, in Arian terms, been created by the Father?

It was on premises such as these that William Ellery Channing preached the famous Baltimore Sermon in 1819 which in many ways became a spiritual declaration of independence of these more liberal thinkers from their more conservative counterparts.

Gradually, many of these Congregational churches in New England began to call themselves Unitarian. Most kept their old legal names such as "The First Parish," or "The First Church." But they often put the word "Unitarian" in parentheses. So powerful was this movement that all of the Congregational churches in Boston became Unitarian in theology except Old South Church. There was even a split in that parish, and the New Old South Church was a split from the Old South Church based upon Unitarian theology. This was the church that the Lemuel Shaws (Elizabeth Melville's family) attended.

So the beginnings of the Unitarian movement were largely intellectual and theological, the giving up of many of the tenets of Calvinism and replacing them with different theological criteria. They did not immediately become "modern" in their religious thinking. For example, Channing argued in the Baltimore Sermon that the Bible was a divinely inspired book, thus retaining the old Protestant Reformation authority of the Scriptures. He just read his Bible in a different way than the Calvinists, and found in the New Testament a basis for belief in one God rather than in the traditional Trinity.

When the American Unitarian Association was formed on 25 May 1825, it was not an association of churches but an association of individuals. Many ministers, for example, were made Life Members of the Association by their congregations who raised the necessary contributions. This Association was conceived primarily as a tract publishing organization for the new, more liberal, ideas.

The next great challenge to Unitarianism came from within the Unitarian movement itself in the person of Ralph Waldo Emerson. Emerson himself had been a Unitarian minister at the Second Church in Boston. He had given up his pulpit purportedly because he did not believe Jesus intended the Last Supper to be commemorated in repeated services of communion. He then became a lecturer and essayist, but he did not completely turn his back on the Unitarian pulpit, and he preached as a supply preacher in Unitarian churches all of the rest of his life.

Emerson had said in the "Divinity School Address" given before the senior graduating class at the Harvard Divinity School in 1838, that the institution of the church had outgrown its usefulness. Men and women should go directly to a mystical communion with the "Oversoul." The reaction to his address, particularly among the faculty at the Divinity School, was strongly adverse. Many believed that Emerson was doing away with the institution of the church, its rites and ceremonies, and its importance.

All students of American literature know that Emerson and many other Unitarian ministers were at the core of what was called the Transcendentalist movement in New England, one of the most significant intellectual movements in this country's history. For some years many Unitarians were strongly influenced by Emersonian idealism.

Twenty-one years later, in 1859, Henry Whitney Bellows, who also was Herman Melville's first minister, went to Harvard and gave his great address called "The Suspense of Faith." Bellows believed that people had suspended their faith in the institution of the church. Bellows was far closer to Ralph Waldo Emerson in many of the facets of his thinking than is generally supposed. But on this issue of the church as an important institution, Bellows wanted a reassertion on the part of religious liberals that the institution of the church really mattered. But he did not want it to be a weak, divided church. He wanted it to be a church with a great deal of diversity so that everyone could feel spiritually at home in a Unitarian church.

Just as the Civil War was ending in 1865, Bellows, almost single-handedly, called a conference of the Unitarian churches of the country to meet in New York City to form an association of churches to work in conjunction with the American Unitarian Association in which membership was not of churches but of individuals.

Out of these meetings a National Conference of Unitarian Churches was formed, and it met for many years in the fall of the year as opposed to the May meetings in Boston of the American Unitarian Association. Bellows proved to be a great denominational organizer. He wanted to include the Universalists in the National Council, but in this endeavor he was discouraged by the laymen because many of them having recently become Unitarians did not want to confuse the issue by introducing another doctrine of Universalism.

By the time of Bellows' death in 1882, Unitarianism had become well institutionalized as another Christian sect. Some of the intellectual leaders had followed the lead of Emerson who was much interested in Eastern religions, and they had begun to speak of the Unitarian faith as something "beyond" Christianity. But in 1885, among the great body of Unitarians, Unitarianism was a very important section of the Christian religion, and confidently many looked forward to the day when Unitarianism would reach almost every man, woman, and child in the United States.

It is very important in our consideration of Herman Melville's action in asking to be enrolled as a member of All Souls Church to realize exactly what the Unitarian religion was like at that time, and especially All Souls Unitarianism. It is such an easy trap (even for historians who ought to know better) to think of Melville's becoming a Unitarian in terms of present-day Unitarianism, but that is patently unfair. Melville did not even join the All Souls of today. He joined it as it was around 1885.

Many today think of Unitarianism as godless, with an informal service, with no rituals, and many other modern practices. But it is only fair and historical to see what kind of a Unitarian Melville became as he finally realized after the skepticism shown in *Clarel* that he had worked his way through his skepticism with a realization of his own humility, and that the human mind can ask more questions, particularly theological ones, than those to which it can give answers. The only way to get authoritative answers to these questions in theology is to posit as authority, the Bible (if we only knew how to correctly interpret it), or to give some religious potentate or assembly or body this same authority.

The Unitarian Church of All Souls in 1885 in true Congregational tradition (it's name was still legally "The First Congregational Church in the City of New York") was governed by the congregation through a board of trustees. Each year to this board, three men (at this time all were men) were elected for three year terms, so that there were nine trustees with staggered terms. But the board of trustees was ultimately responsible to the congregation, and the congregation made all decisions concerning the ordination or the calling of ministers, the content and nature of the worship service (although a lot of this was left to the minister), the budget, etc. Even though some of the church members were individual members of the American Unitarian Association, and the church itself was a member of the National Conference of Unitarian Churches, and sent delegates to its meetings, the church was completely independent. No one in Boston could tell All Souls what to do or not to do, what to believe or not to believe.

In theological matters the church adopted a general covenant which had to be affirmed by those who joined the church. But the covenant was not a creed, and everyone was thoroughly entitled to his own interpretation of such a covenant. The covenant was what bound the members of the church together. But each individual member had the responsibility to make up his mind as to what he himself believed.

Thus when Herman Melville joined All Souls Church, he bound himself to no hierarchy, no creed, Christian or otherwise. He simply agreed to search for the truth and to adopt whatever he believed to be the truth for his own use.

In the period of the early 1880s All Souls was a congregation in transition. Bellows, after a forty-three year ministry, had died early in 1882. The church then valiantly sought to find another younger Bellows. In this they were sorely disappointed for there simply was not another Henry Bellows around. They decided on a very young minister who had been settled for only a year at Winchester, Massachusetts. To "steal" a minister away from a church after such a short settlement, the church needed for reasons of tact to ask the permission of the Winchester church to release their pastor. Having received this permission (What small church could deny the chance for their minister to be the New York preacher?), Williams became the third minister of All Souls.

In 1883, when the young Theodore Chickering Williams came to succeed Bellows, the church was at the height of its importance. It had a large congregation that included many of New York City's "greats." On a Sunday morning Fourth Avenue was lined with the carriages of many of the most prominent people in New York City. Melville's description of the carriages lined up on the street in "The Two Temples" would be an accurate picture of All Souls in the 1880s.

But Theodore Chickering Williams was no Henry Bellows in preaching ability nor in leadership capacity; and gradually the congregation thinned out, so that by 1891, when Melville died, the church was struggling to remain viable, and eventually in 1896, Dr. Williams left to become the headmaster of the Hackley School, a new school in Tarrytown that a New York Unitarian woman had founded.

Because the "List of Persons in Congregation of All Souls Church, New York" is so fundamental to our study of Herman Melville's formal religious affiliation, something ought to be said about this list. When Theodore Williams came to be the minister of All Souls in 1883 the question of membership in the church must have been confusing. Henry Bellows was not a good record keeper, and his list of members has never turned up in any of the extant material in the church archives or in the attic of his vacation home in Walpole, New Hampshire which I personally have ransacked with his granddaughter.

Williams started a membership book, and almost all of the entries are in his writing. As we have seen, this is not a list of pew owners or persons who rented pews. This is a list which according to the bylaws of All Souls constitutes the membership of the "Church" as contrasted with the "Society." The lists of pew owners and renters are to be found in the Treasurer's records in the All Souls archives. Inscribed on the title page of the little book are the words "Corrected up to January 1885." which is two years into Williams' ministry.

There also is another note on the front page of the book which reads, "To be kept in the Communion Table drawer per order Pres[ident] of Board of Trustees." Why the book would be kept in the communion table I do not know, except that it may have been thought to be a safe and convenient place to store the book. Membership in the church was not necessary for a person to take part in the communion service. The bylaws of the church state explicitly that any Christian could partake of the communion. This was an unusually open practice for any Christian church in this period.

The names in the book are all entered in the same hand, and a street address and occasionally a business address are given. There is a page or two for each letter of the alphabet. All told there are the names of approximately four hundred individuals (some of the names are indecipherable, I have counted crossed-out names of those who left the city or were deceased). The woman's first name is usually not entered but is rather included with her husband and reads "Mr. and Mrs." This number means probably that one-half or one-third of the persons affiliated in some way with the society are listed in this membership book of the church.

This list would be a good basis for a study for someone interested in New York City at this period of history. Names *not* in the book are surprising. There is no Mrs. Elizabeth Melville, although Henry Thomas, who married one of the Melville daughters, is listed in the book as living at the Melville's address, but no Mrs. Thomas is listed.

In the 1880s the service at All Souls was actually quite formal. There were litanies, responsive readings, formal prayers, and responses. In many ways the service would today be termed "Low Episcopalian." The minister preached a well-prepared sermon, usually written out except in exceptional circumstances. It was not a simple homily common in many churches. The sermon was considered to be the most important part of the service, and a minister was judged on the content of his sermon as well as the manner of his delivery. Bellows, we are told, used to look up at the ceiling a lot, (which was a long way off) during his prayers and occasionally during his sermons. But he had a powerful voice. When young Williams became the minister, the congregation dropped precipitously, and the emptier the basilica became the worse the acoustics were. His voice reverberated among the empty pews. The church tried a sounding board above the pulpit after Williams came. But it was difficult to hear the young Williams because he did not have the strong voice of Bellows. Eventually he became so distressed with having to become "inspired" each week to deliver a sermon, and as he became depressed the quality of his sermons became poorer.

I have always believed ever since I learned Herman Melville had attended All Souls beginning in 1850 when the family rented a pew, that he and Bellows would scarcely see eye to eye on the basic fundamental matter that bothered Melville so much—the reality of evil. Even though Bellows had founded and served as the president of the United States Sanitary Commission, and thus he had seen the carnage on the battlefields of the Civil War, his personality seemed to leave out human suffering in its deeper aspects. In this matter Melville would scarcely agree. He did not believe with Bellows that the world was evoluting to better things, but that evil was very real and there were no theological answers as to why suffering was allowed by a good God, the problem of theodicy, the problem tackled in the Old Testament book of Job, with no good answers, and tackled again and again by modern writers, with somewhat the same inconclusive results.

Williams was a simpler man, less addicted to causes than Bellows. He was essentially a poet and a writer of the words to hymns. Having read much of his sermonic material, I am not certain that he had much of an answer to the problem of evil. But in the early days when he first came to All Souls, he must have preached inspiring sermons with a lot of preparation. He just couldn't get inspired "on cue," and his preaching lapsed.

When people think of a modern Unitarian church they realize that there is now a communion service in very few Unitarian churches. This was not true in either All Souls or the Church of the Messiah (the other Unitarian church in New York City) which at that time tended to be even "higher church" than All Souls. All Souls had a communion service. It was not the Roman Catholic Mass nor even the typical Protestant communion service. The Unitarians had eliminated the "magic" about the consecration of the elements. They used bread and wine, and they held that it remained bread and wine, and did not become Christ's body, no matter what words were said over them. But the communion service was a reminder of the sacrifice of Jesus for all of mankind, the man who showed men how to live but was put to death by people who did not understand. Since I placed so much emphasis upon the idea of communion as illustrated in the hanging of Billy Budd on the yardarm, we ought to ask about the communion service at All Souls.

We don't know exactly what the communion service at All Souls meant to Herman Melville. But we have quite a definitive view of Mrs. Melville's beliefs. In the second of the two letters which were originally published from the "Henry Whitney Bellows Papers" at the Massachusetts Historical Society, the one to Henry Bellows from Elizabeth Melville is quite revealing about this matter. Mrs. Melville thanked her pastor for his long talk with her "which has been a very great comfort." Then she wrote, "I lay to heart your encouraging words, and pray for submission and faith to realize the sustaining power of the Master's love, and to approach his Table in the very spirit of his last command."

Note that in this sentence both Master and Table are capitalized. This can only mean that Elizabeth is referring to the communion service at All Souls. As has been previously explained, Unitarians at All Souls a hundred years ago belonged to what Bellows called the middle ground of Unitarian theology; that is, they were not Christians in the orthodox sense in believing in the Sacred Trinity. And yet they often (as did Channing) baptized in the name of the Father, Son, and Holy Spirit or Holy Ghost, the three persons of the Trinity.

The All Souls parishioners thought of communion as a celebration of the sacrifice that Jesus made for all humanity by his death on the cross. The communion service emphasized this, and although the elements of bread and wine were not considered to be either actual Body and Blood of Christ or the Essence of the body and blood of Christ, they still used these terms.

They also used the *King's Chapel Prayerbook* for many of their ceremonies. The *King's Chapel Prayerbook* was altered in 1783 by the pastor and wardens of King's Chapel in Boston to take out any references to the Trinity, or so it was claimed. This prayerbook was very much like the Episcopalian Prayerbook on which it was modeled, and when the Unitarians used these words they meant something entirely different than the Episcopalians or members of the Church of England.

George Willis Cooke, a Unitarian historian, wrote:

The last twenty years of the nineteenth century saw an increased use of the simpler Christian rites in Unitarian churches. In that time a distinct advance was made in the acceptableness of their communion service, and probably in the number of those willing to join in its observance. The abandonment of its mystical features and its interpretation as a simple memorial service . . . has given it for Unitarians a new spiritual effectiveness. The same causes have led to adoption of the rite of confirmation in a considerable number of churches.[1]

Cooke also wrote:

The devotional spirit of Unitarians, however, found its most emphatic and beautiful expression in religious hymns and poems. The older Unitarian piety found voice in the hymns of the younger Henry Ware, Norton, Pierpont, Frothingham, Peabody, Lunt, Bryant, and many others.[2]

So Unitarianism at All Souls in 1885 was a modest kind of Christianity although opening up to the validity of other religions. There was a strong belief in God, in Jesus as the Christ, the example, and the Holy Spirit. It was not a religion of the least common denominator which tends to become the order of the day in many of today's churches. The people believed strongly in their church. They only believed that they did not have all of the answers. And I am convinced that this is what made the Unitarian Church of All Souls appealing to Herman Melville. He had been through that excruciating process of believing, as Calvinism taught, that there were answers, and that with enough searching one might find them. But after he wrote *Clarel* he must have grown a bit tired of looking for the white whale of *Moby-Dick*, and he settled down to live out the rest of his life, which was to end in a few short years, with some peace of mind.

It was not that he had not searched for the answers. He had probably searched as assiduously as almost any other human being. He simply was not willing to take short-cuts and jump across the abyss to a belief that he could not find for himself, but must be taken upon authority. So I believe that these last few years when he joined the church are perhaps the most significant years of his life. Instead of just letting the clock wind down, he went through a struggle of the soul which found contentment not in the answers but in having struggled to find the answers, and to realize that we are human beings and not gods. He became intellectually and spiritually humble.

One of the most influential Unitarian thinkers after the Civil War in the intellectual realm was the British preacher and professor, James Martineau. Brother of Harriet Martineau, he became the Unitarian minister at Dublin and then at Liverpool. In 1841 he was appointed professor of mental and moral philosophy at Manchester New College. He left this position for London in 1857 when that institution had made London its new home. He became the pastor also of the Portland Street Chapel. He was one of the most profound thinkers and most effective writers of his day, and his many books greatly influenced American Unitarian thinking during this period, and they can still be found in many ministers' collections and church libraries.

After the Civil War, Martineau indicated that he wanted to make a trip to America to speak and to preach. But like many other Englishmen, he had been sympathetic to the South during the Civil War, and Henry Bellows was strongly against his coming to America. But Bellows' reasons were political not intellectual, for he recognized Martineau as one of the great minds of traditional Unitarian thinkers.

When the fifth minister of All Souls, Dr. William Laurence Sullivan, was a Roman Catholic professor at Thomas College in Washington, D.C., he became quite interested in Martineau's writings. Sullivan began to challenge some of the current thinking in his own church, particularly the propagation of the Papal Infallibility by Pope Pius X in 1907. He made some assignments to his pupils in Martineau's writings, and came under much suspicion from his colleagues. Eventually, Sullivan was sent to a Catholic Mission in Austin, Texas, to think over his theology, and he later begged to be released from his vows. But Martineau's writings were of the depth that interested an intellectual like Dr. Sullivan much more than any writings of his own contemporary American Unitarians.

There is diversity in many church bodies. There are many sects in Christendom. But one particular kind of diversity is to be found in a Unitarian church, and perhaps in a few other Protestant churches of the "free" tradition. This is not a diversity between churches which exists within many Christian denominations. There are "low church" and "high church" Episcopalians, for example. There are many differences within other church bodies. But Unitarianism is one of the few religions which encourages individual diversity within a church. Unitarians believe there is no necessity for all members of a church to think alike for them to worship together. In general, all must assent to a common covenant, but each individual is expressly encouraged to think for himself or herself. This idea of diversity must have strongly appealed to Herman Melville, for he didn't have to agree with Bellows evolutionism, or the concept that things were all getting better and better. If his new minister, Theodore Williams, was a little more sentimental than Melville would himself have been, he did not have to agree with the minister in order to be a good member of the church.

Melville had been brought up in strict Calvinism, and he was supposed to agree with the creeds and the interpretation of the Bible handed down by the minister. There was no such necessity at The Unitarian Church of All Souls. He could be a free spirit, and he could think through every religious problem and come to his own conclusions, and if he did not come to a conclusion, if there were some blurred areas, that too was acceptable.

One would make a mistake to believe that Henry Bellows and All Souls Church represented accurately all or most of the churches which termed themselves Unitarian. There were definitely right and left wings within the denomination. In preparing for the first meeting of the National Conference in New York in April 1865, Bellows made a trip to Boston to address a group of fifty ministers at the Hollis Street Church. He gave a long address on uniting the various wings of the denomination, and this was followed by a three hour discussion among the ministers. He had misgivings about the forthcoming conference from both the conservatives and the radicals: the conservatives not knowing to what they were committing themselves, and the radicals being concerned about any statement of faith, believing that it inevitably became not a covenant but a creed.

When he returned to New York, Bellows wrote to his son Russell about the state of the denomination. There was a first group which he termed "the elder men," and he said that these were the old-fashioned Unitarians "preaching the doctrine of self culture & personal righteousness." He wrote that they were "pretty jealous of anything which don't originate in Boston."

Bellows also found a second group of "radicals." These men were "transcendental in their philosophy, unhistorical in their faith . . . young men just out of Divinity Studies—who really think Xity [Christianity] is only one among a great many other religions." They were fearful that "some test may be applied, some 'creed' slipped around them." Bellows said that they wanted no standard of faith.

There was also a small section of "evangelicals . . . who believe[d] that Jesus Christ was strictly a miraculous person & a savior indeed." A few of the most prominent ministers of Boston belonged in this group.

The fourth group was "another set of Broad Church men." Bellows made it clear to his son, "with this party I belong and am working."[3]

Bellows was somewhat relieved that there would be two laymen present for every minister at the Conference, for the laymen, he believed, might be less opinionated.

This period, of course, is some twenty years before Melville joined All Souls Church. But it probably presents a picture of the denomination which would be fairly accurate at Melville's time. The movements presaged by the Free Religious Association were to develop in the Western Conference (which really should be termed the Mid-Western Conference), and the humanist movement within Unitarianism developed late in the nineteenth century and was very strong in the early twentieth century. But few of these influences in the denomination greatly affected All Souls Church in New York City. In its entire history there has been a middle-of-the-road and not a radical theological emphasis. God is not a dirty word at All Souls as in some Unitarian churches today, and neither humanism nor the Free Religious Movement ever took hold in the church. The ministers have largely been theistic in their beliefs—certainly through the ministry of Minot Simons which ended with his death in 1941. Herman Melville was joining a particular church, not a denomination, and although many of the things for which the denomination stood were also believed by the members of All Souls, many of these influences were never strong in the time that Herman Melville lived.

No one apparently has seriously asked the question as to why Melville, towards the end of his life, should actually want to join the church that he and his family had attended, perhaps sporadically, for so many years after returning to New York City after the thirteen year hiatus at "Arrowhead" at Pittsfield. There was no special reason or outside pressure for Melville to join the church. It is true that his children had been christened by two Unitarian ministers, Malcolm by Henry Bellows, and the other three by Orville Dewey in retirement in Pittsfield. The family rented a pew whenever they could afford it, and one did not have to belong to the church to rent or to own a pew. The communion service was open to anyone who professed to be a "Christian," so one did not need to join the church for that reason. Certainly Mrs. Melville had not brought pressure for Herman to actually join the church, for the records give no indication that she ever joined the church, as Herman did.

Therefore, my suggestion that he joined the church because finally in his later years he had come to be at peace with himself may make some sense. One is apt in one's later years to feel that all of the answers need to be found for every philosophical and theological question that the human mind can conjure up. Melville must have joined All Souls because there were no specific things he had to believe that he didn't already believe. He had made his religious pilgrimage, and it was a pilgrimage typical of many who were raised under Calvinism. The difference was that these questions seemingly bothered Melville more than most thinking people. So one would expect his reaction to be a positive one when he gave up thinking that he had to answer every possible question. He went to his minister, Theodore Chickering Williams, and told him according to the church bylaws that he wanted to be entered in the books as a member of the church. Dr. Williams obliged, and locked in the All Souls safe today is Dr. Williams list of communicants, and Herman Melville's name is so inscribed. This was the final stage in Herman Melville's Religious Journey. ←

C H A P T E R   T E N
IN RETROSPECT

Some of Herman Melville's best literary work is to be found in his short stories. They were written in the depths of his despair after the financial failure of *Moby-Dick*, and they appeared in magazines, in serial form. Melville hoped that these stories would bring him income needed to feed and clothe his growing family while living at their farm "Arrowhead" at Pittsfield in the Berkshires.

One of these that is little known because it was not published in his lifetime is a story titled "The Two Temples." It is interesting for us to consider, for it deals with his own relationship with the institution of the church. The ideas expressed in this short story contrast strongly with his opinions a quarter of a century later when he was writing *Billy Budd*. He became less critical of the church as the years passed, and he finally accepted the church by joining All Souls Church in Manhattan. This is an interesting part of Melville's spiritual odyssey.

At the end of January in 1848, Melville, along with Elizabeth's half-brother, Lemuel Shaw Jr., and his own brother Allan, climbed the steeple of Trinity Church, an appealing way to look down on New York City in those days. It evidently impressed him a great deal for he used the material as "The First Temple" in his short story.

"The First Temple" is a fanciful tale of walking three miles to a stylish church, and being refused a seat. At All Souls and most of the churches of the city, pews were owned or rented by parishioners, and often although the church seemed partially empty, these pews were being reserved for those who owned them or rented them. At All Souls pew owning and renting was not given up until the congregation moved into its present edifice at Lexington Avenue and Eightieth Street in 1932.

Melville wrote, "How disdainful the fat-pouched beadle-faced man [the Sexton, an office of great prestige in New York City churches] looked in answer to my humble petition, he said they had no galleries. Just the same as if he'd said, they didn't entertain poor folks."

Melville remarked about the "noble string of flashing carriages drawn up along the curb." He probably saw the same sort of a row of carriages drawn up on Broadway when he first attended the Church of the Divine Unity, and later at the All Souls Church at Twentieth Street and Fourth Avenue. He wrote about "the gold hat-bands, too, and other gorgeous trimmings."

Slinking through the crowd, he saw a very narrow vaulted door. He believed that this door led to the belfry or steeple. It was unlocked. He ascended some fifty steps up a narrow curving stairway, to a platform. He saw on three sides, three gigantic Gothic windows of richly dyed glass." He felt this place "was only a gorgeous dungeon." Making a little scratch on the glass he could look down and see the congregation on their knees. He pulled his prayerbook from his pocket, and tried to join in the service. But he wrote, "Though an insider in one respect, yet I am an outsider in another."

The text of the minister's sermon was "Ye are the salt of the earth." That little quote is a sideswipe at the makeup of the congregation, for they really believed that they were the salt, and probably the sugar, of the earth also.

The service ended, the people went out. Melville waited until he heard no noise outside the door. He tried to open the door. It was locked. Trapped inside the steeple! Everyone had gone home!

What was he to do? He thought for several hours, and then finally decided that he had to ring the bell. He gave the rope a slight pull. Nothing happened. Then he gave a heavy pull, and something mechanical started the bell ringing with a loud series of peals. The Sexton (the beadle-faced man) soon came running and opened the door. He threw Melville out of the church with no kind words, and handed him over to two policemen who had been summoned by the ringing of the bell. Eventually Melville paid a fine and was sent home.

It is a good yarn, and evidently when Melville visited the steeple of Trinity Church with Lemuel Shaw Jr. and Allan, he put a lot of impressions in his mind which he never forgot.

"The Second Temple" takes place in London on a cold Saturday night. The man who is telling the tale (presumably Melville, for it is narrated in the first person) is completely strapped for cash. He wants to get in out of the cold, but the churches are not open. He finally locates a theater where a great actor is playing that night. He has no money for a ticket. But standing outside during the intermission, a man hands him a red ticket for readmission. Melville goes up many flights of stairs. Finally he emerges at the highest gallery, where all the poor of London who could afford a ticket are seated. He likes his companions, the play, and the great actor.

He goes home to his lonely lodging. He could not sleep thinking of the First Temple and the Second Temple, and concludes the story with these lines.

"Thinking of the First Temple and the Second Temple, and how a stranger in a strange land I found sterling charity in the one, and at home, in my own land, was thrown out of the other."[1]

This simple story illustrates Melville's attitude towards churches in the most depressed period of his life. In retrospect we can look back at this anti-institutional attitude and compare it with Melville's attitude towards the institution of the church almost thirty years later when his attitude had evidently changed considerably.

How did this change come about? It was not a deathbed repentance and acceptance of some religious authority so that he could make his peace with God. Melville was somewhat like Henry David Thoreau, who on his deathbed is rumored to have responded to the minister's query as to "whether he had made his peace with God?" Thoreau is reputed to have answered that "he and God had never quarrelled."

Melville unlike Transcendentalist Henry Thoreau had quarrelled with God. Throughout his life, Melville had tried to work his way from the vengeful God that he had learned about in his early Dutch Reformed Church upbringing. He did not blame God even for the tragedy of the white whale's sinking of Captain Ahab's ship and the death of all of the crew except the teller of the tale, one Ishmael.

I have in my video library a copy of an early black and white movie made from the story of *Moby-Dick* in which in the last scene, Ahab, alive and well, returns to the Spouter's Inn, alone in the middle of the night, to be welcomed home by his wife. The makers of this cinema certainly did not catch the meaning of Ahab's monomaniacal quest to kill the white whale, and instead in his eagerness to kill the whale, the ship and all of its hands, except Ishmael, went down in the cruel sea, while in *Moby-Dick*, Ahab was last seen lashed to Moby-Dick.

We have seen that Melville even made a trip to the Holy Land hoping that there he might find the answers to some of his philosophical and theological queries. But he was also disappointed in this search. He must have realized as he grew older and more mature that one can ask a lot of questions, and that possibly there may not be answers to them that humans will ever understand.

So he matured in his later years in his attitude about the church as an institution. He did not join All Souls because it gave him all of the answers to these queries that his fertile imagination had asked. But All Souls Church encouraged him to seek, even if he didn't find, all of the answers. And my impression is that instead of just wasting away until death came to him, that he adjusted his thinking to the fact that the mysteries of the universe may remain just that, and like an alcoholic he turned to life one day at a time, and his impatience with God grew less, and he accepted more, even some human institutions that he had formerly ridiculed.

There was almost no mention of Herman Melville's passing in the New York newspapers. Theodore Chickering Williams, the minister of All Souls, conducted a simple funeral service at the home at 104 East 26th Street. Very few persons attended the services. Most of Dr. Williams personal papers have never been found, and perhaps he spoke from notes or extemporaneously, or simply conducted a simple service from the prayer book. The eulogy was given by Titus Munson Coan, a friend.

Herman Melville eventually emerged from the shadows of obscurity with the publication of Raymond Weaver's biography in 1920, almost three decades after his death. Then the scholars put together *Billy Budd*, and Melville literally was resurrected from obscurity.

Did he die then as many have said as a man who carried his disillusionment and skepticism to the grave? Or did he die having realized that the human mind can ask more questions than it can ever answer, and that try as we will with all of our might, we are never going to know all of the answers to all of the questions that were asked in *Clarel*. Many of them may be mysteries forever, and unanswerable. Like Job, he believed that he might never understand, but he trusted, and he gained humility.

I believe that Melville found some peace in his heart and mind, and that having struggled with his Calvinistic upbringing all of his life and passing through a period of rejection of that system of thought, and disillusionment and skepticism, that at the end he found in the Unitarian religion something which allowed him the freedom of no religious creeds, something that he could honestly intellectually and spiritually accept, and something which gave a soul that had been tortured so long "a peace that passeth human understanding." Thus, Herman Melville's religious journey was completed, and in words as obscure yet as meaningful as Melville himself often used, his fellow Unitarian, Ralph Waldo Emerson, wrote to explain the ultimate mystery:

> "What is excellent,
> As God lives, is permanent:
> Hearts are dust, heart's loves remain;
> Hearts love will meet thee again.
> House and tenant go to ground
> Lost in God, in Godhead found." *(Thenrody)*

N O T E S

PREFACE:
1. Jay Leda, *The Melville Log: A Documentary Life of Herman Melville*, Gordian Press, New York, 1969, Vol. 1., xi.
2. Ibid, xiv.
3. George Willis Cooke, *Unitarianism in America*, ASMS Press, Inc., New York, 1902, Reprint 1971, 412-475.

CHAPTER ONE: *"Born Into Religious Controversy"*
1. After his father's death in 1832, his son, Gansevoort Melvill, changed the spelling of his name to *Melville*, and the immediate family did likewise. When referring to the Herman Melville family in this volume we shall use the latter spelling, even though in his early years Herman Melville spelled his name without the final "e."
2. Leyda, *The Melville Log*, Vol. 1, 3.
3. Ibid, 4.
4. I am much indebted for material about the religious background of the Melville family to T. Walter Herbert, Jr. *Moby-Dick and Calvinism*, Rutgers University Press, New Brunswick, New Jersey, 1938, 38.
5. Ibid, 39-40.
6. Mumford, *Herman Melville*, The Literary Guild of America, New York, 1929, 11.
7. Herbert, *Moby-Dick and Calvinism*, 31.
8. Ibid, 29.
9. Mumford, *Herman Melville*, 14.
10. Ibid, 15.
11. Education in America was very different during the nineteenth century from what it has become today. Children spent their early years in grammar school learning principally the three R's, after which the young of the socially elite were given some form of secondary education, usually, when the children were about ten years of age. College was entered somewhere between the ages of twelve and fourteen. Children who did not receive secondary education and or college were usually apprenticed out to artisans to learn a trade.
12. Edward Tanjore Corwin, *A Manual of the Reformed Church in America*, revised, New York, 1869, 43.
13. Ibid, 44.
14. Herbert, *Moby-Dick and Calvinism*, 36-37.
15. Ibid, 37.
16. *Sermons by the late Rev. J. S. Buckminster*, Boston, Massachusetts, 1816, 44. Published by his Parishioners.
17. Leyda, *The Melville Log*, Vol. 1, 51.
18. Herbert, *Moby-Dick and Calvinism*, 46.
19. Ibid, 46.
20. Ibid, 51.
21. Herbert, *Moby-Dick and Calvinism*, 45.
22. Leyda, *The Melville Log*, Vol. 1, 53.
23. Herbert, *Moby Dick and Calvinism*, 59.

CHAPTER TWO: *"Disillusionment"*

1. Herman Melville, *Redburn,* 173, Doubleday Anchor Books, Doubleday & Co., Garden City, New York, 1957, 173.
2. Ibid.
3. Ibid.
4. Ibid.
5. Ibid, 173-174.
6. Ibid, 174.
7. Ibid, 175.
8. Ibid, 179.
9. Ibid, 180.
10. Ibid, 180-181.
11. Herman Melville, *Moby-Dick,* Northwestern University Press and The Newberry Library, Evanston and Chicago, 1988, 41-48.
12. Gay Wilson Allen, *Melville and His World,* Viking Press, New York, 1971, 47, (Picture of the *Acushnet* log).
13. Herman Melville, *Typee,* Signet Books, New American Library, 1964, 27.
14. Allen, *Melville and His World,* 61.
15. Probably for Melville it was a matter of hours rather than days to reach the Typee Valley, and he probably remained there for only a few weeks.
16. *Typee,* 146-147.
17. Allen, *Melville and His World,* 64.
18. From the "Afterward" by Harrison Hayford, New American Library Edition of *Typee,* New American Library, Inc., New York, 1964, 314.
19. Herman Melville, *Omoo, A Narrative of Adventure in the South Seas.* L. C. Page & Co., Boston, 1892, 191-192.
20. Ibid, 198.
21. Ibid, 161.
22. Ibid, 162.
23. Ibid, 161.
24. Ibid, 198.
25. Ibid, 199.
26. Ibid, 198-199.
27. Melville, *Typee,* 222.
28. Ibid, 144.
29. Ibid, 145.
30. Ibid, 145.
31. Ibid, 145.
32. Ibid, 225.
33. Ibid, 223.
34. Ibid, 223-224.
35. Ibid, 224-225.

CHAPTER THREE: *"Melville and Social Idealism"*

1. Herman Melville, *White-Jacket,* Northwestern-Newberry Edition, Northwestern University Press & The Newberry Library, Evanston and Chicago, 1970, 134.
2. Ibid, 135.
3. Ibid, 137.
4. Melville to Hawthorne, June (1) 1851, Quoted in Leyda, *The Melville Log,* Vol. 1, 189.

5. Leyda, *The Melville Log*, 196.
6. Ibid, 209.
7. Ibid, 210.
8. Ibid, 324.
9. Ibid, 246.
10. Ibid, 302.
11. Ibid, 265.
12. Ibid, 275.
13. *Daily Evening Transcript* (Boston), 5 August 1847, Quoted in Leyda, *The Melville Log*, Vol. 1. 255.
14. *The Melville Log*, Vol. 1, 255.
15. c.f. Kring, *Liberals Among the Orthodox*, Beacon Press, Boston, 1974, 74-91 a complete account of this church building.
16. Allan Nevins and Milton Halsey Thomas, (eds.) *The Diary of George Templeton Strong*, New York, Macmillan, 1952, Vol.1, 267.
17. Leyda, *The Melville Log*, 276-277.
18. Melville, *Typee*, Vol. 1, 276-277. Leon Howard Historical Note 291, Quoted in Sealts, *Melville's Reading, Revised and Enlarged Edition,* University of South Carolina Press, 1988, 3.
19. Sealts, *Melville's Reading*, 4.
20. Ibid, 46.
21. Mattheissen, *American Renaissance*, 122.
22. Sealts, *Melville's Reading*, 4.
23. Ibid, 46.
24. Melville, *Redburn*, 174.
25. Leyda, *The Melville Log*, 360.
26. Melville, *White-Jacket*, 138.
27. Ibid, 140.
28. Ibid, 141.
29. Ibid, 143-144.
30. Ibid, 141.
31. Ibid, 146.
32. Ibid, 157.
33. Ibid, 155.
34. Ibid, 155-156.
35. Ibid, 156.
36. Ibid, 156.
37. Ibid, 158.

CHAPTER FOUR: *"Reality As Symbolic Allegory"*
1. Herman Melville, *Mardi*, Modern Reader's Library, College & University Press, New Haven, Conn. 1973. From the *Introduction* by Tyrus Hillway, 5.
2. Leyda, *The Melville Log*, Vol. 1, 5.
3. Ibid. 298.
4. Mattheissen, *American Renaissance*, 378.
5. Hillway, *Introduction to Mardi*, 5.
6. Weaver, *Herman Melville, Mariner and Mystic*, 274.
7. Ibid, 278.

8. Merrill R. Davis, *Mardi, A Chartless Voyage*, Yale University Press, New Haven, Conn. 1952.

9. Edwin Haviland Miller, *Melville*, George Brazillier, Inc., New York, 1975, 142

10. *Encyclopedia Britannica*, 1959 Edition, "*Allegory*."

11. Mumford, *Herman Melville*, 102.

12. Ibid, 102-103.

13. Ibid, 103.

14. Melville, *Mardi*, 515.

15. Mattheissen, *American Renaissance*, 383.

16. Melville, *Mardi*, 516.

17. Ibid, 522.

18. Hillway, *Introduction to Mardi*, 12.

19. Ibid, 13.

20. Ibid, 13.

21. Ibid, 13.

22. Miller, *Melville*, 149.

23. Mattheissen, *American Renaissance*, 381.

CHAPTER FIVE: *Humanism and Allegory: Moby-Dick*

1. Leyda,*The Melville Log*, 365.

2. Ibid, 365-366.

3. Ibid, 371-372.

4. Herbert, *Moby-Dick and Calvinism*, 171.

5. The text quoted here from Chapter 9 of *Moby-Dick* is based upon the critical edition of Melville's works, the Northwest-Newberry Edition. It was prepared by Harrison Hayford, Hershel Parker, and Thomas Tanselle.

6. Curtis Dahl, *The Seaman's Bethel and Its Chaplains*, The New Bedford Port Society, New Bedford, Mass. 1979, 14.

7. Ibid, 15.

8. Ibid, 15.

9. Ibid, 16.

10. Ibid, 14.

11. Ibid, 14.

12. Ibid, 14-15. Anyone interested in the full story of Father Taylor told by two of his devoted followers is referred to Rev. Gilbert Haven & Hon. Thomas Russell, *Father Taylor, The Sailor Preacher*, B. B. Russell, Boston, 1872.

13. Mattheissen, *American Renaissance*, 179.

14. Ibid, 180.

15. Ibid.

16. Ibid. 183.

17. Leyda, *The Melville Log*, 430-431.

18. Ibid, 431.

19. Ibid.

20. Ibid, 434.

21. Ibid, 437.

22. Ibid.

23. Ibid.

24. Ibid, 439.

25. Ibid.

CHAPTER SIX: *"Disillusionment With Human Nature"*
1. Allen, *Melville and His World*, 107.
2. Herman Melville, (Henry A. Murray. editor), *Pierre or the Ambiguities*, Hendricks House, New York, 1957, xiv.
3. Ibid.
4. Ibid, xv.
5. Ibid, xvii.
6. Ibid, xx.
7. Ibid. xxx.
8. Ibid.
9. Mumford, *Herman Melville*, 252.
10. R. V. B. Lewis, (Editor), Signet Classical Edition of *The Confidence Man*, New American Library, New York, 1964, "Afterward," 265-266.
11. Ibid, 266.
12. Weaver, *Herman Melville, Mariner and Mystic*, 17.

CHAPTER SEVEN: *"The Depths of Skepticism and Clarel"*
1. Herman Melville, *Clarel* (Walter E. Bezanson An "Introduction,") Hendricks House, New York, 1960, x.
2. Herman Melville, *Clarel*, Hendrick's House Edition, New York, 1960, 523.

CHAPTER EIGHT: *"The Last Years, The Christ Figure, and Billy Budd"*
1. Weaver, *Herman Melville, Mariner and Mystic*, 381.
2. William Ellery Sedgwick, *Herman Melville, The Tragedy of Mind*, Harvard University Press, Cambridge, Massachusetts, 1944, 246.
3. Ibid, 248.
4. Ibid, 249.
5. Miller, *Melville*, 358.
6. Ibid, 358-359.
7. Ibid, 366.
8. Ibid, 369.
9. Ray B. Browne, *Melville's Drive to Humanism*, Purdue University Press, Lafayette, Indiana, 1971, 370.
10. Ibid, 371.
11. Ibid.
12. Ibid, 378.
13. Ibid, 379.
14. Ibid, 394.
15. Paul McCarthy, *The Twisted Mind, Madness in Herman Melville's Fiction*, University of Iowa Press, Iowa City, Iowa, 1990, 125.
16. Ibid.
17. Ibid, 127.
18. Ibid, 142.
19. Mumford, *Herman Melville*, 351.
20. Ibid, 351-352.
21. Ibid, 352-353.

22. *The Endless Winding Way in Melville, New Charts by Kring and Carey*, Donald Yannella and Hershel Parker, (Editors), The Melville Society, Glassboro, New Jersey, 1981. This booklet contains pictures of the relevant documents at the Unitarian Church of All Souls, New York City, taken by Donald Yannella.

23. c.f. Kring, *Henry Whitney Bellows*, Appendix B, "Church Membership Criteria," Skinner House, Unitarian Universalist Association, Boston, 1979, 479-481.

c.f. Kring and Carey, "*Two Discoveries.*"

c.f. *The Writings of Herman Melville*, Vol. 14., *Correspondence*, Northwestern Newberry Edition, 857-860.

24. Lawrance Thompson, *Melville's Quarrel With God*, Princeton University Press, Princeton, New Jersey, 1952.

25. The history of All Souls Church from 1819-1978 is well documented in a trilogy by Walter Donald Kring, *Liberals Among the Orthodox, Unitarian Beginnings in New York City, 1819-1839*, Beacon Press, Boston, 1974; *Henry Whitney Bellows*, Skinner House, Unitarian Universalist Association, Boston, 1979; *Safely Onward*, All Souls Church, New York, 1991.

26. Herman Melville, *Billy Budd, Sailor*, (Hayford and Sealts, eds), University of Chicago Press, Chicago, 1962, 4. and Plate II.

27. Ibid, 132.

CHAPTER NINE: "*Unitarianism in 1885: All Souls Church*

1. George Willis Cooke, *Unitarianism in America*, 240.

2. Ibid, 243-244.

3. Henry W. Bellows to Russell N. Bellows, March 1, 1865, in "The Bellows Papers," Massachusetts Historical Society.

CHAPTER TEN: "*In Retrospect*"

1. Jay Leyda, (Editor), *The Complete Stories of Herman Melville*, Random House, New York, 1952, 149-165.

I N D E X